Joshua

BOOKS IN THE BIBLE STUDY COMMENTARY SERIES

BIBLE STUDY COMMENTARY

Joshua

PAUL P. ENNS

ZONDERVAN
PUBLISHING HOUSE
OF THE ZONDERVAN CORPORATION
GRAND RAPIDS, MICHIGAN 49506

To Helen
whose faith, love, and optimism
has encouraged me
in the ministry

JOSHUA: BIBLE STUDY COMMENTARY
Copyright © 1981 by The Zondervan Corporation
Grand Rapids, Michigan

This printing August 1981

Library of Congress Cataloging in Publication Data

Enns, Paul P., 1937-
    Joshua, Bible study commentary.

    Bibliography: p.
    1. Bible. O.T. Joshua—Commentaries.   I.   Title.
BS1295.3.E54   222'.207   81-11530
ISBN 0-310-44041-6   AACR2

Edited by John Danilson and Edward Viening

Printed in the United States of America

83   84   85   86   87   88 — 10   9   8   7   6   5   4   3   2

Contents

Introduction

A. Title of the Book

The Book of Joshua is the first book in the second division of the Hebrew canon called the Prophets. Within this category it is listed among the books of the former prophets, comprising Joshua, Judges, Samuel, and Kings. The Book of Joshua derives its name from the principal character within the book.

The name Joshua means "Yahweh saves" or "Yahweh is salvation." The name is suitable, since God used the successor of Moses to conquer the land of Canaan, subjugate the enemies, and give the nation its inheritance.

B. Authorship

Contrary to what proponents of the documentary hypothesis say, it may safely be asserted that the Book of Joshua is the product of a single author and is a literary unit.[1] Several factors provide guidance in discussing the authorship:

1. Numerous parts of the book indicate they were written by an eyewitness (5:1; 5:6; 15:4).[2] Other detailed descriptions indicate an

---

[1] Evangelical scholars generally conclude that the book was basically written by Joshua, with minor additions after his death, cf. G. L. Archer, *A Survey of Old Testament Introduction* (Chicago: Moody Press, 1964), pp. 252-253; John J. Davis, *Conquest and Crisis: Studies in Joshua, Judges, and Ruth* (Grand Rapids: Baker, 1969), pp. 22–23; Merrill F. Unger, *Introductory Guide to the Old Testament* (Grand Rapids: Zondervan, 1951), pp. 281-283.

[2] Unless otherwise indicated (e.g. by context), references refer to the Book of Joshua when the Bible book is not given. Direct Bible quotations are from the New International Version unless specified otherwise.

eyewitness (cf. the sending out of the spies, chap. 2; crossing the Jordan, chap. 3; capturing Jericho and Ai, chaps. 6-8; the deceit of the Gibeonites, chap. 9; and the victory at Gibeon, chap. 10).

2. The book indicates an early authorship. Canaanite cities are mentioned by their archaic names (cf. 15:9, Baalah for Kiriath Jearim; v. 13, Kiriath Arba for Hebron; v. 49, Kiriath Sannah for Debir). A date prior to the twelfth century is evident since Sidon is mentioned as "Greater Sidon" (cf. 13:4-6; 19:28). The Jebusites were still inhabiting Jerusalem, which thereby necessitates a date prior to David.

3. At least parts of the book were written by Joshua. The explicit statement in 24:26 says, "And Joshua recorded these things in the Book of the Law of God." In 18:9 we find a hint of Joshua's authorship of at least that part of the book.

4. Certain details in the book cannot be ascribed to Joshua's authorship, the notable example being the account of his death (24:29-30).

The book may be regarded as essentially the work of Joshua with minor additional details recorded by Eleazar or Phinehas.

C. Date of the Conquest

1. *1 Kings 6:1*

This passage is important in establishing an Exodus date of 1446 B.C. from Egypt. The passage indicates that Solomon began to build the temple in the fourth year of his reign, which was 480 years after the Israelites came out of Egypt. Since Solomon began his reign in 970 B.C., his fourth year was 966 B.C. Adding 480 to 966 indicates a 1446 B.C. Exodus date. Since Israel wandered in the desert for forty years (Num. 14:34), the date that Joshua and the Israelites began their conquest of the land was 1406 B.C.

2. *Judges 11:26*

Jephthah indicates that Israel had possessed the land and lived in it for 300 years from the conquest until Jephthah's day. The succeeding chronology to the fourth year of Solomon adds up to approximately 144 years, which agrees in substance with 1 Kings 6:1 and further substantiates a 1406 B.C. invasion.[3]

---

[3]The 482 years are arrived at by suggesting the following chronology: Exodus to Heshbon, 38 years; Heshbon to Jephthah, 300 years; remainder of Jephthah, 5 years; Samson, 40 years; Eli, 20 years; Samuel, 20 years; Saul, 15 years; David, 40 years; Solomon, 4 years. Cf. Unger, *Introductory Guide*, p. 289.

3. *Archaeological evidence*

The archaeological data points to the early date of 1406 B.C. for the conquest of Canaan by the Israelites. John Garstang excavated Jericho from 1930 to 1936 and unearthed pottery relating to the reign of Amenhotep III (1414-1378), but there was no pottery from Akhenaton, Amenhotep III's successor. Since Garstang's work, there has been considerable debate over the interpretation of his findings, a principal opponent of Garstang being Kathleen Kenyon, who excavated Jericho from 1952 to 1958. Much of Garstang's work is nonetheless defensible and provides added support for the view of an early date for the conquest.[4]

D. Date of the Writing of the Book

The date of the writing of the book is related to the authorship. Since the majority of the book was written by Joshua, a suggested date for the major part of the book is c. 1375 B.C. with the completion c. 1370 B.C.

E. Historical Setting

While the Book of Joshua is a literary unit distinct from the Pentateuch, it follows and resumes the narrative of the Israelites where it terminated with the Book of Deuteronomy. The Book of Joshua describes the Israelites' advance into the Promised Land, their conquest of the city-states, and the distribution of the land among the tribes.

The Amarna letters reveal that the Book of Joshua accurately portrays the historical situation during this period. The letters represent the country as divided into small feudal city-states that were often at war with one another. Extant Amarna letters from Jerusalem, Gezer, Lachish, Jarmuth, and Eglon request help from Egypt because of the "Habiru" invaders (a possible identification with the Hebrews). The cities that correspond with Egypt (Megiddo, Ashkelon, Acco, Gezer, Jerusalem) were conquered later by Israel, while the cities not corresponding with Egypt were conquered early.[5] Thus these letters, written between 1400 and 1367 B.C. by the Canaanites to the Egyptians, help

---

[4]Leon J. Wood discusses the issue in some detail, positing the conclusions of Garstang as well as the reactions of Kathleen Kenyon. He concludes that the theses of Kenyon do not totally abrogate the conclusions of Garstang. Cf. Wood, *A Survey of Israel's History* (Grand Rapids: Zondervan, 1970), pp. 94-99.

[5]Although problems remain in the discussion of the identification of the "Habiru," there is adequate support for suggesting an association between them and the Hebrews. Cf. Archer, *Survey of Old Testament Introduction,* pp. 266-271, for discussion and his affirmative conclusion.

provide information concerning the historical circumstances at the time of the conquest.

The Ras Shamra (Ugaritic) tablets reveal the licentious and degrading nature of the Canaanite inhabitants, with their chief emphasis on fertility and sex. Their idolatrous practices of child sacrifice and temple prostitution would have been spiritually contaminating to the Israelites; hence, severe measures of extermination were commanded by God.

F. Promise of the Land

The conquest of the land of Canaan by Joshua and the Israelites is based on the Abrahamic covenant. In Genesis, where God begins dealing with mankind, we find that He gave man a responsibility on several occasions, but each time man failed. There are three major failures in the early chapters of Genesis: the Fall in Eden, apostasy before the Flood, and the failure at Babel. God left off working directly with the world in general, and in Genesis 12 He began to work with a special people. From this point on God deals with mankind through the Hebrews. He called them to be a nation, and this calling of the Jews began with a promise to Abraham called the Abrahamic covenant (Gen. 12:1-3), and three promises are involved in this covenant:

1. *Promise of a land* (Gen. 12:1)

God called Abraham from Ur "to the land" that He would give him. This was an unconditional promise God was giving to Abraham and his posterity, and it is further developed in the Palestinian covenant (Deut. 30).

2. *Promise of a seed* (Gen. 12:2)

God promised Abraham that He would make a great nation of the patriarch, indicating a great posterity for him. The ultimate fulfillment of this aspect of the Abrahamic covenant is through the Davidic covenant (2 Sam. 7:16) in which Messiah rules over His people, the Jews.

3. *Promise of a blessing* (Gen. 12:3)

This promise to Abraham finds fulfillment in the new covenant (Jer. 31:31-34). This involves a spiritual blessing to the Jews and, through the Jews, to the world.

These covenants have not yet been fulfilled but look to a future fulfillment at the return of Christ and the establishment of the millennial kingdom.

Israel's occupation of the land of Canaan relates to the promise that God gave to Abraham inasmuch as it indicates Israel's *right* to the land. This right to the land and the unconditional nature of God's promise are seen in a number of passages. In Genesis 13:14-17 God reaffirmed the Abrahamic covenant with no conditions attached. He said He was giving the land to Israel unconditionally—it was to be Israel's land forever (v. 15). Abraham was to confirm the covenant by the shoe covenant—by walking on the land in order to appropriate what God had given him in the transacted agreement (v. 17).

In Genesis 15:17-21 God ratified the covenant with Abraham through a formal ritual involving blood. In this type of agreement the two parties would slay an animal, split the carcass in two, and lay the halves aside; the parties would then walk together between the split halves to confirm the covenant. The ritual normally indicated both parties were bound by the covenant, that is, that it was a bilateral agreement. In this case, however, it was a *unilateral* agreement—it was binding on God alone.

In the case of God giving the land to Abraham, the Lord caused a sleep to come on Abraham. God, manifest in the Shekinah glory, passed between the halves alone (Gen. 15:17). This indicated that the covenant was binding only on God's part. He alone was to be responsible for the fulfillment of the promise to give the land to Abraham.

The dimensions of the land are given in Genesis 15:18-21. It was from the "river of Egypt"—either the Nile or a wadi to the east of the Nile—to the Euphrates River.

Genesis 17:19 establishes the Jews as the rightful heirs to the land of Palestine. There the promise is given to Isaac instead of Ishmael. The continuation of the promise is through the posterity of Isaac but not through Ishmael.

When Joshua led the Israelites into Canaan, he was obeying God's command to take the land that had been given to them. Israel was about to appropriate the land that had been promised to their patriarch, Abraham. But they failed in this quest to appropriate the land, and fell into idolatry. Thus, while the land remains Israel's, the appropriation of the land awaits future fulfillment when Messiah removes the blindness from Israel's eyes.

G. Purpose of the Book

The purpose of the Book of Joshua is to show how God faithfully led the nation, which He had brought into existence, into the Promised Land. In this sense the book develops the unfolding of God's purpose and dealing with His people, Israel, and we note that His dealing with Israel as recorded in the Pentateuch continues in Joshua. In Genesis God promised that Abraham would be the father of a nation, while in Exodus the nation was formed and given a constitution that is elaborated on in Leviticus. Numbers records the forty years of wandering, Israel's sin of unbelief in the desert (chap. 14), and their resultant judgment. Because Israel refused to believe that God could bring them into the land when the spies went through the land, God judged them at Kadesh Barnea. That generation perished in the desert, and only Joshua and Caleb, the stalwarts of faith, entered the land. Deuteronomy relates the restatement and interpretation of the Law for the benefit of the new generation that would enter the land under Joshua's leadership. Thus the faithfulness of God in establishing His people in the land, according to His promise, is clearly depicted in the Book of Joshua.

H. Outline of the Book

There are four major parts to the Book of Joshua. Part One: Invasion of the Land (1:1–5:15) describes the preparations for the conquest of the land; Part Two: Subjection of the Land (6:1–12:24) describes the actual conquest of the land in the central, southern, and northern campaigns; Part Three: Distribution of the Land (13:1–22:34) describes in detail the division of the land between the twelve tribes of Israel; Part Four: Conclusion (23:1–24:33) narrates Joshua's concluding exhortations to the nation in the land.

Part One: Invasion of the Land (1:1–5:15)
    Chapter 1: Commission of Joshua (1:1-9)
        A. The Promise (1:1-5)
        B. The Provision (1:6-9)
    Chapter 2: Preparation for Conquest (1:10–2:24)
        A. Mobilization of Israel (1:10-18)
            1. Command of Joshua (1:10-15)
            2. Response of the people (1:16-18)
        B. Mission of the Spies (2:1-24)

PART ONE: INVASION OF THE LAND

Chapter 1

Commission of Joshua
(Joshua 1:1-9)

In Genesis 12 God unconditionally called Abraham and his physical descendants to a land that He would give them as an inheritance. Israel had never appropriated the land under the patriarchs, so now God was working on behalf of Israel to bring them into the land under the leadership of Joshua. While biblical prophecy indicates that Israel will not fulfill the Abrahamic covenant until the second advent of Christ, the initial phase of Israel's appropriation of the land was about to take place under Joshua.

A. The Promise (1:1-5)

Because of the sin of unbelief at Kadesh Barnea (Num. 14), God ordained that the generation of Israelites that left Egypt would not enter the land. Instead, their judgment by the Lord was that they would have to wander in the desert for forty years. Not even Moses, who also had disobeyed God, would enter the land. But there were two men, Caleb and Joshua, who had believed that God would give them the victory, and because of their faith they would enter Canaan with the new generation of Israelites. But who would lead the people? Moses, the man commissioned by God (Exod. 3), was the only leader the people had known.

The opening section of the Book of Joshua (1:1-9) is important inasmuch as it shows that Joshua was appointed by God to become the new leader of the nation Israel. This opening section forms the preamble to the Book of Joshua and links it to the Pentateuch by the opening words, "After the death of Moses" (v. 1). The nation had mourned the death of Moses for thirty days (Deut. 34:8), and that period had now come to an end. The departed Moses is designated in 1:1 as "the servant of the LORD" (cf. 24:49). This was an honorable title used also to designate kings (1 Kings 8:66; 2 Kings 8:19), and it is found in the Ras Shamra texts as a royal title. "It thus denotes a leader of the sacral community, especially in his sacral function as mediator of the Covenant in the cases of Moses and Joshua."[1]

Joshua's relationship to Moses is established at this point. He is "Moses' aide," or, literally, Moses' minister. This refers to "official rather than menial service."[2]

The Lord had previously appointed Joshua as Moses' successor (Num. 27:18–23). Now, following the death of Moses, God confirms Joshua as the successor to Moses. The call of Joshua was to be clear to both Joshua and the people.

Israel was encamped at Shittim (cf. Num. 25:1; Josh. 2:1; 3:1), east of the Jordan River opposite Jericho. God commanded Joshua, "You and all these people . . .cross the Jordan River into the land I am about to give to them" (1:2). The challenge facing Joshua was an invitation to faith just as it had been previously for Moses. As Israel departed from Egypt, God called on Moses to trust Him to lead the people across the Red Sea; when Israel was ready to enter Canaan, God called on Joshua to trust Him to lead the people across the flooding Jordan River. This was clearly a call to faith but the venture of faith rested on the fact that God had given them the land. "Into the land I am about to give to them" repeats in veiled terms what God had frequently and candidly promised Israel (Gen. 12:1–3; 13:14–17; 15:18–21). The explicit promise is repeated in 1:4.

In 1:3 God promises to be with Joshua "as I promised Moses." The statement again reaffirms Joshua as Moses' successor. Moreover, God was giving the entire land to the Israelites, "not excepting a single foot's breadth."[3] The background to this promise is Deuteronomy 11:18–25. God's statement, "I will give," views the land as irrevocably belonging to the nation of Israel; in that sense the promise of the land was unconditional. The appropriation, however, was to be conditioned on obedience (Deut. 11:22–23), and biblical prophecy indicates that a

---

[1] John Gray, *Joshua, Judges and Ruth* in *The Century Bible* (Greenwood, S.C.: Attic Press, 1967), p. 49.
[2] Hugh J. Blair, "Joshua," *New Bible Commentary: Revised* (Grand Rapids: Eerdmans, 1970), p. 235.
[3] C. F. Keil and F. Delitzsch, *Joshua, Judges, Ruth* in *Biblical Commentary on the Old Testament* (Grand Rapids: Eerdmans, 1968 reprint), p. 29.

repentant and obedient nation ultimately will inherit the land. The effects of disobedience are seen in Judges and elsewhere in the Old Testament.

The specific dimensions of the land that Israel is to inherit are given in 1:4. The term "desert" designates the southern border as the arid region south of the Dead Sea. "From Lebanon" refers to the northern boundary that penetrates Syria and perhaps specifically refers to Mount Hermon, which as part of the northern territorial boundary would have been visible from Shittim. The northeastern border is determined by the Euphrates River, while the western boundary is the "Great Sea"—the Mediterranean.

The Hittites are mentioned in 1:4 as holding the territory eastward, and this is one of the forty times that the Bible mentions the Hittites. Prior to 1906 there was no evidence outside the Bible that these people actually existed, and so critics asserted that the Bible was in error since there was no supporting archaeological evidence. But in 1906 Professor Hugo Winckler of Berlin discovered some 10,000 clay tablets at Boghazkeui (modern Turkey), which turned out to be the ancient Hittite capital. "This vast store of inscriptional material revealed the Hittites to be not only an important people of the ancient world, but a people of an extended empire."[4] The Hittite empire, which existed from about 1900 B.C. to 1200 B.C., was an enormous territory, ranging from south of the Black Sea eastward to the Euphrates River.

In 1:5 the Lord encourages Joshua through several promises: (1) He promises Joshua victory—"no one will be able to stand against you all the days of your life." The same promise was given to the entire nation earlier (Deut. 11:25). (2) He promises Joshua His presence—"I will be with you." This promise explains why Joshua would be assured of continual victory—victory was connected to God's abiding presence. Moreover, not only would God be present with him, but God also promised him, "I will never leave you," literally, "I will not drop you." The word "as" reappears in 1:5 (cf. 1:3; 3:7), reassuring Joshua that just as He had been with Moses and did not fail or forsake him, so He would be with Joshua, never to fail or forsake him. At this promise, Joshua's thoughts probably turned to the recent past when God had given the Israelites victory over Sihon, king of the Amorites, and Og,

[4]Merrill F. Unger, *Archaeology and the Old Testament* (Grand Rapids: Zondervan, 1954), p. 92.

king of Bashan (Num. 21:21–35). God was promising Joshua military success as they entered the Promised Land.

B. The Provision (1:6–9)

God had promised Joshua success on Israel's entry into the land; now He was calling for obedience and courage in the outworking of His promise. "Be strong and courageous" suggests that Joshua is to rally his heart in obedience to the Lord's injunction and is to take possession of the land. The exhortation to "be strong" is given repeatedly (1:6–7, 9). (1) Be strong because of God's promise (1:6). (2) Be strong because of God's law (1:7). (3) Be strong because of God's presence (1:9).

The responsibility of Joshua rested on a faithful adherence to the law of God, which had been prominent in Moses' earlier injunctions (Deut. 5:29; 28:14). In fact, the lengthy statement of Deuteronomy 28 reminded Israel that there was blessing in obedience to the law, but chastisement for disobedience. The term "law" can be used in a variety of ways. It can be used to designate the Ten Commandments (Exod. 20:1–17). It can refer to the entire Pentateuch—the first five books of the Old Testament (perhaps its most normal usage, cf. Deut. 31:9, 11). The term can also refer to the entire Scriptures (Matt. 5:18). In Joshua 1:7–8 the term "law" designates the Pentateuch. The Israelites were to obey the law that had been mediated through Moses and expounded in the Book of Deuteronomy (cf. Deut. 1:1, 5; 4:44; 6:1 et al.), and faithful obedience to God's law would ensure their success.

To assure their success, Israel was to constantly meditate on the law. The term "meditate" means to "recite in an undertone." The equivalent Greek word was used to denote "the meditative pondering and audible practice of orators."[5]

A suitable synonym for meditate would be reflection. Fay says meditation is

> a mature reflection upon the law by which Joshua penetrates more deeply into its meaning, and thus becomes qualified to speak more clearly, pointedly, and powerfully to the people.[6]

The meditation on the law is to be "day and night" (cf. Ps. 1:2), which is an idiom meaning continually. Continual meditation would result in obedience to the law, which in turn would ensure success.

---

[5]John Rea, "Joshua," *The Wycliffe Bible Commentary* (Chicago: Moody Press, 1962), pp. 207–208.

[6]F. R. Fay, "The Book of Joshua" in *Lange's Commentary on the Holy Scriptures* (Grand Rapids: Zondervan, 1960 reprint), p. 42.

The opening phrase of 1:9 is a reminder that this venture into Canaan is God's doing and not Joshua's. God had commanded him; it was at God's directive that the people were to go forth to take the land. That being the case, God promised to be with His people. The assurance of His presence would give them victory. The statement "Do not be terrified; do not be discouraged" stands as the antithesis of "Be strong and courageous!" Positively, Joshua is to be strong; negatively, he is not to be afraid. The reason is that God is with him!

For Further Study

1. Describe in detail what constitutes success according to 1:1–9.

2. Read an article on Joshua in a Bible dictionary or encyclopedia.

3. Read an article on the word "law" in a Bible dictionary or encyclopedia. What different ways is the term used?

4. Establish a plan for yourself whereby you will faithfully meditate daily on the Word of God.

Chapter 2

Preparation for Conquest
(Joshua 1:10–2:24)

Preparations were now being made for the assault on Canaan. The fighting men were mobilized and spies were sent into the land in preparation for the invasion.

A. Mobilization of Israel (1:10–18)

1. *Command of Joshua* (1:10–15)

In his first act of preparation for the invasion, Joshua commanded the "officers of the people." It was their duty

> as the keepers of the family registers, to attend not only to the levying of the men who were bound to serve in the army, but also to the circulation of the commands of the general, to issue orders to the people in the camp to provide themselves with food, so that they might cross the Jordan within three days, and take the land that was promised them by God.[1]

The function of these officers was twofold: (1) They issued the orders drafting men into the army; (2) They acted as staff officers, issuing the commands of the superior.

The officers were to go through the camp and command the people to prepare provisions for themselves in preparation for crossing the Jordan River. Joshua's intention was to cross the Jordan "three days from now" (1:11). The mention of three days is listed three times in this general context (1:11; 2:22; 3:2), but it is not entirely clear how these passages are to be understood.

One view is that the spies' mission delayed the original plan; if so, the spies were sent out simultaneously with the command for preparation (1:11). The spies spent one day traveling to Jericho and three days

---

[1]Keil and Delitzsch, *Joshua, Judges, Ruth*, p. 31.

hiding in the hill country (2:22). Following their return, Israel set out from Shittim to the Jordan. They encamped east of the Jordan for another three days before they actually crossed over (3:2). If this is correct, Joshua's original plan was delayed.

An alternative view is that the spies were sent out prior to 1:11 so that the account of chapter 2 is parenthetical. The statement of 3:2 would then be seen as synonymous with the command of 1:11. In this case, the crossing actually occurred within three days.

The tribes of Reuben and Gad and the half-tribe of Manasseh had already determined to remain on the east side of the Jordan. In Israel's conquest of the Transjordan, the lush cattle country became available to Israel (Num. 21). The two-and-a-half tribes petitioned Moses to give them this land as their inheritance (Num. 32:1–5). Moses complied with their request but laid down certain conditions (Num. 32:20–32; Deut. 3:18–20). Moses stipulated that the two-and-a-half tribes must fight alongside their brothers on the west side of the Jordan until the land was taken. It was this stipulation of Moses that Joshua had in mind when he commanded the two-and-a-half tribes. Ultimately about 40,000 men from Reuben, Gad, and the half-tribe of Manasseh fought alongside their brothers (4:13). Since Numbers 26:7, 18, 34 indicates there were about 110,000 men in these two-and-a-half tribes, the 70,000 men must have remained at home to protect the women and children. The 40,000 called "fighting men" (1:14 KJV: "mighty men of valour"; NASB: "valiant warriors"), probably represented the best fighting men from the eastern tribes. The same Hebrew expression is rendered "fighting men" in 6:2 but is "best fighting men" in 8:3 and 10:7.

The Israelites would go forward "fully armed" (1:14 NASB: "in battle array"). The Hebrew term is probably related to an Arabic cognate meaning "five" or "five-formation." This denotes the formation of the army that would enter and invade Canaan: it would have a center, vanguard, rearguard, and two wings.[2] The army would advance thus:

VANGUARD

WING   CENTER   WING

REARGUARD

The term citing this formation is seen again in 4:12.

---

[2]Gray, *Joshua, Judges and Ruth*, p. 52.

2. Response of the people (1:16-18)

The two-and-a-half tribes agreed to the command of Joshua; they were willing to go to war on behalf of their brothers. They also recognized the authority and leadership of Joshua, acclaiming him as successor to Moses. Their response in 1:17–18 reflects a similarity to the words of God in 1:5–6. God had promised Joshua that He would be with him as He had been with Moses; that was the expressed desire of the tribes (1:5, 17). God had commanded Joshua to "be strong and courageous" (v. 9); that was the wish of the tribes.

B. Mission of the Spies (2:1-24)

1. The spies' commission (2:1)

The Israelites were encamped at Shittim, only about fourteen miles from Jericho. Shittim lay seven miles east of the Jordan River and Jericho seven miles west of the Jordan. Shittim lay in the foothills of the eastern edge of the Jordan Valley and is also referred to as Abel Shittim (Num. 33:49), which means "stream of the Acadia trees." The location was ideal, for it lay between two streams of water flowing out of the hills into the Jordan. The site has been identified as Tell al-Hammam, between the two watercourses known as Wadi Kufrein and Wadi Hisban.[3]

In preparation for the invasion, Joshua sent two men as spies to investigate the land, "especially Jericho" (2:1). The location of Jericho was strategic: the city had an abundant water supply and lay in a valley serving as a main entrance into the land. The oasis had afforded an important water supply for generations, Jericho having been continuously occupied and fortified since 7000 B.C.[4] Jericho was situated in the Jordan Rift Valley, a natural fault line that follows the Jordan River and runs south into Africa. The natural depression varies from being very narrow to perhaps twelve miles in places. It affords mild winters and is a generally lush area. The plain in which Jericho lay would mark an important entry point into the land; it would enable Israel to gain a major foothold as they advanced. They would march westward from Jericho, slicing the land in two, and then strike southward and northward in their conquest.

The men were sent "secretly" (2:1), probably because of the problem

---

[3]Denis Baly, The Geography of the Bible (New York: Harper & Row, Publishers, 1974), p. 202.
[4]Gray, Joshua, Judges and Ruth, p. 54.

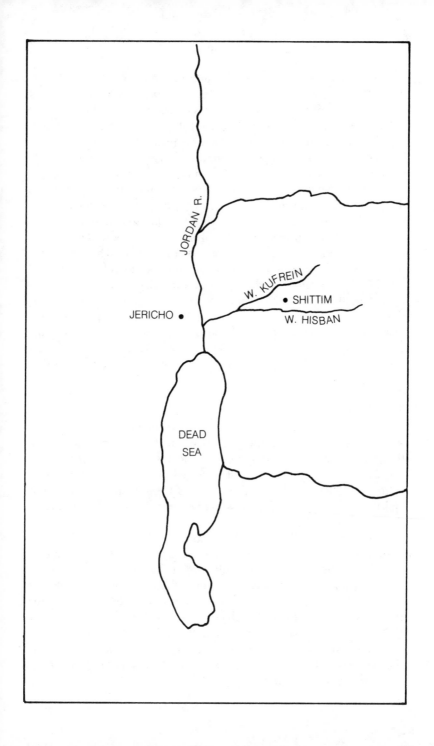

created when the spies were sent into Canaan from Kadesh Barnea (Num. 13–14) and the people heard the report publicly and expressed their fear and unbelief. This secret mission was carried out to avoid any recurrence of the unbelief that occurred at Kadesh Barnea. The second reason for the secrecy of the mission was to prevent the Canaanites from hearing about it. The Israelites were only fourteen miles away, and the Canaanites were edgy because of the presence of this vast horde.

When the spies came to Jericho, they entered the house of Rahab the prostitute. This was due to several reasons: (1) They would attract very little attention. Anyone entering that household would not be looked upon with suspicion; (2) Rahab's house was located on the wall of the city and afforded an easy and secretive exit. The spies could quickly escape from the city because of the location of the house (cf. 2:15); (3) The outcome of the visit was a manifestation of the grace of God. A public outcast and a sinner was nonetheless one through whom the grace of God could be revealed. Rahab is held up in the New Testament as a heroine of faith (Heb. 11:31). Even more astonishing is the fact that Jesus Christ was a descendant of Rahab (Matt. 1:5). The things that are despised by men are used mightily by God for His glory (cf. 1 Cor. 1:27–29).

2. The spies' concealment (2:2–7)

The enormous number of Israelites, encamped just fourteen miles away, alarmed the Canaanites. Thus when the king of Jericho heard that two men had entered the city, he became upset. Like other Canaanite kings, he was the ruler of a city-state, not of an extensive land area. These independent city-states were common at the time, and this lack of political unity would hasten the downfall of Canaan at the onslaught of Israel.

Informants told the king of the spies' visit to Rahab. The king's emissaries converged on Rahab's house, demanding that the spies be turned over to them. Rahab admitted that the spies had come to her, but she professed ignorance concerning their identity. She informed the officials that the men had left the city at dusk when the main gate of the city was being closed. Rahab exhorted the men of Jericho to pursue the spies, but she had hidden them in the stalks of flax on the roof. The flat roofs were used for a great variety of purposes, one of which was drying crops. Since flax in Palestine grows to a height of three feet, it was not difficult to hide the spies.

Rahab's lie was intended not only to remove all suspicion from herself and any conspiracy with the Israelites, but also to prevent any further search for them in her house and ultimately to prevent their capture.[5] Several points should be noted concerning Rahab's lie. Was the lie justifiable in God's sight?

(1) The fact that a lie is always a sin is taught in both the Old and New Testaments (Exod. 20:16; 23:1; Eph. 4:25). (2) If lying would be acceptable in this case, then a case for situation ethics could be established. That being the case, there would be no control or limitations on any moral standard. Who or what would set the standard when a lie would be considered acceptable? (3) Rahab seems to have been an immature believer who assumed that the end justified the means. Both Joshua and the New Testament confirm that she was a believer (Heb. 11:31; James 2:25), yet Scripture does not justify any lie by a believer. Rea has shown that Rahab was reflecting a prevalent attitude of those days. "In Oriental ethics, guarding one's guest as an act of hospitality is one of the highest virtues."[6] Thus it was not uncommon for people to lie (cf. Gen. 12:13; 20:2; 26:7; 1 Sam. 19:14; 27:8–12; 29:6–8), and had definitely become a problem at that time.[7] (4) God commended Rahab for her faith but not for her sin. Having recognized the messengers as sent from God, Rahab responded in faith and received physical salvation when destruction came to Jericho. However, she was saved despite her lie, not because of it. She should have so regulated her speech that, on the one hand, she did not lie and, on the other hand, she did not reveal the location of the spies' hideout. (5) God is sovereign and could have protected the spies even if Rahab told the truth. (6) As a further option, God may have allowed the spies to die when the truth was told. Believers must represent the truth at all times and allow God to take care of the situation.[8] A case in point would be Daniel's three friends (Dan. 3:17–18).

3. *The spies' conversation* (2:8–21)

    a) *The faith of Rahab* (2:8–14)

After the departure of the king's men on their false mission, Rahab went up to the roof to speak to the spies (2:8). She acknowledged her faith in the God of Israel, recognizing that God had given Israel the

---

[5]Keil and Delitzsch, *Joshua, Judges, Ruth*, pp. 34–35.
[6]Rea, "Joshua," p. 208.
[7]Davis, *Conquest and Crisis*, p. 35.
[8]Ibid.

land, and she explained that the terror of the Israelites had fallen on
them (v. 9). The pronoun "us" refers to all the Canaanites in the land
rather than merely the people of Jericho. The terror of the Canaanites
is probably to be connected with the Song of Moses (Exod. 15:1–18).
Following Israel's victory over Pharaoh and his armies at the Red Sea,
the people of Israel had sung this victory song. It spoke of Pharaoh's
armies going down into the sea. It also spoke prophetically of the fear
that would come to the Canaanites when they would hear of it, and
now Exodus 15:15–16 was being fulfilled in the time of Rahab.

The terror was specifically connected to two events described in
2:10. The Canaanites had heard how the Lord had divided the waters
of the Red Sea (Exod. 14:21–25). By a mighty miracle He had caused
those waters to stand up in two enormous walls, opening a gap probably half a mile wide so that the Israelites could walk through on dry
ground. The second event was the defeat of the Amorite kings, Sihon
and Og, and the victory over the kings is described in Numbers
21:21–35.

The Amorite kingdom was relatively new, having been established
only a generation previously by military adventurers who had come
down from Syria.[9] The Amorites were not a localized people. One
group settled in the area later occupied by Judah (Deut. 1:19f.; Josh.
10:5f.); another group represented the two kingdoms of Heshbon and
Bashan on the east side of the Jordan River, extending in an area well
below the Dead Sea to an area north of the Sea of Galilee (cf. Num.
21:13f.; Josh. 2:10; 9:10; 24:8; Judg. 10:8; 11:19f.).[10]

Having been previously refused passage through Edom, Moses led
the Israelites around Edom and Moab, coming to the eastern border of
Sihon, king of the Amorites (Num. 20:14f.). When Sihon also refused
Israel passage through her territory, a battle ensued at Jahaz (Num.
21:23). Sihon was decisively defeated by the Israelites, who captured
all the cities and villages of Sihon, including Heshbon, and lived in
them (v. 25). The kingdom of Sihon was divided between Reuben and
Gad, the southern border of Reuben being the Arnon River and the
northern border of Gad the Yarmuk River.

The primary reason Reuben and Gad chose to stay east of the Jordan
was their desire to continue the pastoral life. They had a large number

⁹John Bright, "Joshua," *The Interpreter's Bible* (New York: Abingdon Press, 1969),
p. 137.
¹⁰H. A. Hoffner, Jr., "Amorites," *The Zondervan Pictorial Encyclopedia of the Bible*,
Merrill C. Tenney, gen. ed., vol. 1 (Grand Rapids: Zondervan, 1975), p. 143.

of livestock and saw that the land was suitable for their herds (Num. 32:1f.).[11] In time, the beautiful pastoral land of Gilead became fairly synonymous with Gad. Yet the borders between Gad and Reuben were not clearly defined as the Reubenites in particular remained partially nomadic. In fact, various families apparently crossed into Palestine to Judah and Benjamin.[12]

The defeat of Og, briefly stated in Numbers 21:33-35, is further elaborated on in Deuteronomy 3:1-11. Of particular interest is the size of Og's bed, which has led to interesting speculation. Deuteronomy 3:11 declares that Og "was left of the remnant of the Rephaites. His bed was made of iron and was more than thirteen feet long and six feet wide. It is still in Rabbah of the Ammonites." The size of the bed suggests Og was a giant. This may also be the reason for the encouragement of the Lord, "Do not be afraid of him" (Deut. 3:2). Some have suggested the phrase "Og . . . was left of the remnant of the Rephaites" indicates he may have been the last of the race of giants. Deuteronomy 2:10, 20-21 indicates these giants existed from patriarchal days and were given various local designations.[13]

In 1918, Gustav Dalman discovered a dolmen—a tall, oval stone that also is called a megalithic grave. The discovery was made in Amman, Jordan, which may well be the actual site of Rabbath-Ammon. The dolmen corresponded nearly to the size of Og's bed. Over one thousand of these hard, gray-black, basalt stones may be found in the general area[14] and the basalt ore could be found all over the area.[15]

Og's capitulation was complete, for Moses stated, "At that time we took all his cities. There was not one of the sixty cities that we did not take from them—the whole region of Argob, Og's kingdom in Bashan" (Deut. 3:4). The conquest of this area was thus completed with all the cities being captured. The human population was annihilated and the spoils of the cities, including livestock, were taken as booty (Deut. 3:6-7). The half-tribe of Manasseh received the kingdom of Bashan, the territory north of the Yarmuk River, as their inheritance.

---

[11]George Adam Smith, *The Historical Geography of the Holy Land* (London: Hodder & Stoughton, 1910), p. 383.

[12]Yohanan Aharoni, *The Land of the Bible* (Philadelphia: Westminster Press, 1967), pp. 189-190.

[13]Elmer Smith, "Numbers," *The Wycliffe Bible Commentary* (Chicago: Moody Press, 1962), p. 131.

[14]Werner Keller, *The Bible As History* (New York: Bantam Books, Inc., 1956), pp. 157-158.

[15]Baly, *Geography of the Bible*, p. 213.

Israel's great victories over Sihon and Og had precipitated fear in the hearts of the Canaanites. Rahab responded with a genuine statement of faith, saying, "The LORD your God is God in heaven above and on earth below" (2:11). Rahab expressed her faith, not in a general God, but in a specific God, the God of the Hebrews. She used the term "LORD" which is Yahweh, the Hebrew covenant name for God (cf. Exod. 3:14-15).

Rahab begged the spies to confirm by an oath that her family would be spared in the coming invasion. She reminded the spies that she had shown "kindness" (Hebrew *hesed*—loyalty) to them. On that basis she asked for a reciprocal loyalty on their part—and that it be bound by a "sure sign." In 2:14 the spies give the equivalent of an oath to her, adding the first of three conditions that would be spelled out in verses 18-20. In the oath

> they pledged their life for the life of Rahab and her family in this sense: God shall punish us with death if we are faithless, and do not spare thy life and the lives of thy relations.[16]

b) *The salvation of Rahab* (2:15-21)

Rahab's house was built on the city wall; hence, she was able to aid the escape of the spies by letting them down on the outside wall by a rope (2:15). She warned the spies to go up into the hill country and hide for three days from pursuers (v. 16).

> The mountains referred to are probably the range on the northern side of Jericho, which afterwards received the name of Quarantana (Arab. Kuruntul), a wall of rock rising almost precipitously from the plain to the height of 1200 or 1500 feet, and full of grottoes and caves on the eastern side. These mountains were well adapted for a place of concealment; moreover, they were the nearest to Jericho.[17]

The mountains (Quarantana) are likely the same place where Jesus was tempted by the devil (Matt. 4:1-11).

The men reminded Rahab that they would be free of their oath to her unless she fulfilled three conditions. (1) She was to tie a scarlet cord in the window of her house (2:18). The cord would identify the house, and Israelite soldiers would pass by the house during the invasion. The thought is reminiscent of Exodus 12:13: "When I see the blood, I will pass over you." Many expositors, the early church fathers in particular, understood the scarlet thread to be a picture of the work

---

[16]Keil and Delitzsch, *Joshua, Judges, Ruth*, p. 37.
[17]Keil and Delitzsch, *Joshua, Judges, Ruth*, pp. 38-39.

of Christ on the believer's behalf. The condition imposed on Rahab demanded a response of faith. The cord that had helped the spies escape was to be the very cord that Rahab would tie in the window. The cord that resulted in the salvation of the spies was also to be the cord that would result in the salvation of Rahab and her family. (2) She was to gather her parents, brothers, and sisters into her house (2:18). They would be saved only by remaining in Rahab's house. Whoever ventured outside would be put to death, but that one's death would be self-caused; the Israelites would not be responsible (v. 19). (3) Rahab was to keep the spy mission a secret (v. 20). This third condition repeats the thought given previously (v. 14).

Rahab accepted the conditions outlined by the men (2:21). Her faith and obedience to the conditions are immediately seen in her action: "she tied the scarlet cord in the window." Hebrews 11:31 commends Rahab as a heroine of faith who trusted God.

4. *The spies' conclusion* (2:22–24)

The spies followed the advice of Rahab. They hid in the mountains for three days; then they returned to their home across the Jordan and related their mission to Joshua. One element of the spies' report is mentioned in 2:24, indicating the spies told Joshua of the Canaanites' dismay in hearing of Israel's triumphs in crossing the Red Sea and in defeating Sihon and Og. No doubt the spies also reported on the physical layout of the land and the entrance and layout of the city of Jericho. Israel was at the threshold of a great triumph!

For Further Study

1. Study a map showing Canaan at the time of the invasion under Joshua. Locate the cities, rivers, and regions mentioned in Joshua 1–2. Familiarize yourself with them.

2. Read an article on the Amorites in a Bible dictionary or Bible encyclopedia.

3. Explain the ingredients of Rahab's faith. What was the evidence of her faith?

4. Look up as many references to "faith" in a concordance as you can. What do you learn about faith from these references?

5. What practical application of faith can you make in your own life?

Chapter 3

Procession Across the Jordan
(Joshua 3:1-17)

A. Organization for the Crossing (3:1-4)

Israel faced a crisis with the flooded Jordan River before them; yet Joshua demonstrated great faith in God's ability to enable this great gathering of God's people to cross the river. Under Joshua's leadership the Israelites marched from Shittim to the eastern side of the Jordan, a distance of seven miles, and encamped at the Jordan in preparation for the crossing.

The Israelites remained at the edge of the Jordan for three days.[1] This, no doubt, was necessary to enable them to make provisions for such a large contingent of people and families to cross the swollen stream. But the delay also taught Israel to wait for God's direction (Ps. 27:14). How could this large company of people cross the Jordan without God's help? In the springtime the normally narrow river flooded its banks so that it filled its depression valley that was 150 feet deep and as much as a mile wide.

During the time of waiting, officers went through the camp and commanded the people to follow the ark of the covenant that the priests carried. The people were further commanded to keep a distance of three thousand feet from the ark. The purpose of this is stated in 3:4: "Then you will know which way to go." Keil and Delitzsch explain:

> The ark was carried in front of the people, not so much to show the road as to make a road by dividing the waters of the Jordan, and the people

---

[1]See previous discussion under 1:11 concerning the "three days." It is possible that these are two distinct events. Cf. Keil and Delitzsch, *Joshua, Judges, Ruth*, pp. 31, 40.

were to keep at a distance from it, that they might not lose sight of the ark, but keep their eyes fixed upon it, and know the road by looking at the ark of the covenant by which the road had been made, i.e., might know and observe how the Lord, through the medium of the ark, was leading them to Canaan by a way which they had never traversed before, i.e., by a miraculous way.[2]

Had the mass of people thronged around the ark, the way in which the people were to travel would have been obscured.

A secondary consideration, while not mentioned in the text, can be assumed. The ark signified the presence of God, for it was there He would meet the people through the mediator (Exod. 25:22). Moreover, when the ark rested, it was established in the Holy of Holies, which no one could enter apart from the high priest on the Day of Atonement. The injunction for the people to keep three thousand feet from the ark was therefore a further reminder of the holiness of God.

B. Consecration for the Crossing (3:5–13)

In preparation for the crossing, Joshua issued a command: "Consecrate yourselves, for tomorrow the LORD will do amazing things among you" (3:5). The word "consecrate" is the frequently used Hebrew word *qadash* that has the basic thought of "be set apart; consecrated." Priests, for example, consecrated themselves through purification (Exod. 19:22; 2 Chron. 29:5, 15, 34; 30:3, 15, 24 et al.). Joshua 7:13 records another incident in which the people consecrated themselves.

The consecration was specifically necessary to prepare the people for the miracle that God would perform among them, showing them that He was with Joshua just as He had been with Moses. Consecration before a major event was not unusual. God called for Israel's consecration when He revealed Himself to them at Sinai (Exod. 19:10–15). On that occasion the consecration took the form of washing their garments. Prior to God's blessing of Jacob, the Lord called for Jacob's consecration. Jacob then instructed his entire household to put away their foreign gods, purify themselves, and change their clothes (Gen. 35:2). This event was a spiritual purification.

> It consisted in spiritual purification also, i.e., in turning the heart to God, in faith and trust in His promise, and in willing obedience to His commandments, that they should lay to heart in a proper way the miracle of grace which the Lord was about to work in the midst of them.[3]

---

[2]Keil and Delitzsch, *Joshua, Judges, Ruth*, p. 41.
[3]Ibid.

At the command of Joshua, the priests carried the ark ahead of the people, indicating that God, as Israel's King, was leading the theocratic nation into the Promised Land. Just as the Lord had led the previous generation out of Egypt by the cloud and pillar of fire (Exod. 13:21), so now He was leading the new generation into the land through His presence in the ark of the covenant.

"Today" would be significant for both Joshua and the nation as the day that God would exalt Joshua before the people (3:7). The miraculous crossing of the Jordan would be a sign to the nation that God was with Joshua *as* He had been with Moses. In that way God would exalt Joshua in the sight of all Israel. The thought is similar to that of 1:2–9. "Today" marks the beginning of God's working on behalf of Joshua.

The priests were commanded to stand in water at the edge of the Jordan (3:8). They were to remain there with the ark until they received further direction. God then revealed to Joshua the manner in which the crossing was to be made (3:9–13); in turn, Joshua explained the manner of the crossing to the people. The miraculous crossing of the Jordan would be the first in a series of signs.

Joshua began by summoning the nation to hear God's directive (3:9). The reason God gave the sign of the parting of the Jordan and then the signs following that would enable the Israelites to defeat their enemies was to cause them to "know that the living God is among you" (3:10). As a result, they would be enabled to defeat seven great nations that were greater than Israel itself (Deut. 7:1). The seven great nations consisted of the peoples inhabiting the land at the time of the invasion.

The *Canaanites* had their origin in Canaan, son of Ham (Gen. 10:15–19). They were a Semitic people that normally lived along the coast of Phoenicia. The general term Canaanites denotes those dwelling along the coast in contrast to the Amorites, who lived in the central hill country. The *Hittites* may have been migrants from the Hittite kingdom in Asia Minor, since that kingdom did not extend as far south as Canaan. These Hittite migrants then established independent city-states in Canaan. The *Hivites* are an obscure people, and are listed as descending from Canaan (Gen. 10:17). The inhabitants of Gibeon were Hivites (Josh. 9:3, 7). Some scholars suggest the Hivites and Horites are actually the same people. Little is known concerning the *Perizzites*, a name that seems to be a general term equivalent to the Amorites. The term *Girgashite* is also obscure, and information about these people is lacking. The *Amorites* were the most powerful race in Palestine, next to the Hittites.[4] They lived on both sides of the Jordan, being replaced on the eastern side by Reuben, Gad and the half-tribe of Manasseh. They also lived in the hill country of Judah on the western side of the Jordan. They were a nomadic people, being a mixture of Northwest Semitic and Hurrian. The *Jebusites* had occupied Jerusalem, previously known as Jebus, and were defeated by David in his capture of the city (2 Sam. 5:6–10). Together, these tribes controlled a considerable territory; but it was this territory that God was now giving to Israel.

The words of the Lord that Joshua conveyed to the people were designed to encourage them; hence, the Israelites were reminded that the God who was leading them in battle was "the LORD of all the earth" (3:11, 13). The designation anticipated the conquests of the nations of the earth. The conquest of Canaan prefigures the final great battle when the Lord will manifest Himself as the Lord of all the earth as He smites the nations (Rev. 19:11–16).

At this point Joshua instructed the Israelites to select twelve men, one from each tribe (3:12). The purpose for this is not stated now, but will be told later (4:2f.). The twelve were to gather memorial stones.

Finally, Joshua explained how the miracle of the Jordan crossing would take place (3:13). The moment the feet of the priests touched the waters of the Jordan, the river would stand up like a wall, just as the Red Sea had done for the nation Israel under Moses (Exod. 14:21). Thus 3:13 explains the "as" statement of verse 7. As Moses parted the Red Sea with the rod, so now Joshua would part the waters of the Jordan through the instrumentality of the ark. The result at the Jordan would be the same as at the Red Sea—the exaltation of the Lord's mediator before the people.

C. Completion of the Crossing (3:14–17)

The march of the people was in all likelihood similar to the Red Sea crossing. A number of people exceeding two million could have marched in a square, one thousand abreast (approximately one-half mile wide) and two thousand deep (less than two miles in length). It would have required about an hour for them to pass over their own length.[5]

---

[4]Unger, *Archaeology and Old Testament*, p. 93.

[5]See the helpful discussion concerning the size of the Exodus and other problems related to the desert wanderings in John J. Davis, *Biblical Numerology* (Grand Rapids: Baker Book House, 1968), pp. 58f.

CANAAN
BEFORE THE CONQUEST

HITTITE EMPIRE

BASHAN
Kingdom of Og

Sidonians

Yarmuk R.

• EDREI

Canaanites

C A N A A N

A M O R I T E S

Hivites

SIHON

Jabbok R.

JERICHO •

Jebusites

• JEBUS

AMMON

• HESHBON

Arnon R.

Kenites

MOAB

Amalekites

EDOM

The narrative indicates that there was more than simply a small passage that opened for the Israelites. When the priests' feet touched the water, the river "piled up in a heap a great distance away" (3:16). The waters of the Jordan pushed back to the town of Adam, fifteen miles north of the crossing point, and the water remained dammed up. The location of Zarethan is unknown. The water that had been flowing into the Salt Sea (i.e., Dead Sea) emptied into that sea; hence, there was dry passage from the town of Adam to the Salt Sea, a distance of more than twenty miles.

The priests stationed themselves in the middle of the riverbed and the people crossed in a large group, probably accomplishing the crossing in half a day. The Israelites' crossing "on dry ground" (3:17) took place in the spring at a time when that entire area normally was flooded. The Jordan River flooded a narrow depression strip, called the Zor, a valley up to a mile in width. Because of this annual flooding, the Zor was rich in vegetation, and lions lived in the valley in ancient times. It was known as "the pride of the Jordan" (Zech. 11:3 NASB). Above the Zor lay the main part of the Jordan Valley, called the *Ghor*. This was also part of the depressed area and extended up to fifteen miles in width. Due to the meager rainfall, much of the area was desert.[6]

In interpreting the crossing, some scholars have understood the event in the light of natural circumstances. For example, on December 7, 1267, the Jordan was dammed for about ten hours at ed-Damiyeh due to the fact that some of the high banks of the Jordan collapsed and fell into the riverbed. Again on July 11, 1927, a landslide occurred in the same area, causing a stoppage for 21½ hours. The major problem, of course, is that these stoppages did not occur during the flood season. It would have been impossible to dam the Jordan during that time.

Clearly, the better solution is to understand the Jordan crossing as a miracle. There are a number of reasons for suggesting this event was a miracle by God on Israel's behalf: (1) The Bible treats the crossing as a miracle. There is a definite emphasis on the fact that the crossing occurred when the Jordan overflowed its banks (3:15). (2) The exact time the crossing occurred also points to the miraculous. Precisely when the priest's feet touched the water, the flow of the water stopped (vv. 15–16); similarly, when the priests' feet left the water on the other

---

[6]Aharoni, *Land of the Bible*, p. 31.

side—at exactly that moment—the water resumed flowing (4:18). This obviously was not a mere coincidence and should not be explained from that standpoint. (3) The river was at flood stage and could not have been dammed up at that time—certainly not long enough for such a large contingent of people to cross. (4) The emphasis is also on the fact that the Israelites crossed the river "on dry ground"—mentioned twice in 3:17. The same Hebrew word is used to describe the miracle of the Red Sea crossing in Exodus 14:21. (5) The inhabitants of the land understood the crossing in terms of a miracle (5:1). Only a miracle wrought by almighty God could have brought two million men, women, and children across the flooded Jordan River.

For Further Study

1. Read an article on the Jordan Valley in a Bible encyclopedia or historical geography of the Holy Land.

2. Why do some people find it difficult to believe in the miracles recorded in Scripture?

3. How can you best be prepared for a major crisis in your life?

4. Consider the term "consecrate" and cite specific ways in which you can turn your heart to God in faith and trust.

5. Reflect on the past year and consider the evidences showing how God has demonstrated His faithfulness to you.

Chapter 4

Commemoration of the Memorial Stones
(Joshua 4:1–5:1)

A. Purpose of the Memorial Stones (4:1–7)

Joshua 3:14–17 gave the general account of the Israelites' crossing; now in chapter 4 some specific details in conjunction with the crossing are given. While 3:17 gave the completion of the crossing, chapter 4 looks back to the placing of the memorial stones, which event took place while the priests were still standing in the riverbed.

The twelve men, one from each tribe, were originally mentioned in 3:12, but the purpose for their selection was not stated at that point. Now in 4:2f. the purpose for selecting these men is given. They represented the twelve tribes of Israel, and the memorial related to the entire nation.

Joshua summoned the twelve men according to the command of the Lord, ordering each man to take up one stone from the dry riverbed where the priests stood on dry ground. The fact that the men carried the stones on their shoulders indicates their fairly large size. They were to "put them down at the place where you stay tonight" (4:3). This is later identified as Gilgal (v. 20), which became the base of Israel's operation within the land.

The stones were to be a sign to future generations (4:6–7). The use of signs as didactic devices is also seen elsewhere in Scripture. Aaron's rod was a sign to rebels (Num. 17:10). In the millennial kingdom thornbushes will be replaced by pine trees and briers by myrtle trees as a sign to the nation of Messiah's blessing (Isa. 55:13). Blood was a sign when the Passover was instituted (Exod. 12:13); God pledged that no plague would fall on Israelite homes marked with blood. Specifically, the sign of the memorial stones served several purposes: (1) It was a witness of God's faithfulness in bringing the nation into the land of Canaan. (2) It was a sign to future generations of what God had done. It was the Oriental way of continually handing down important teachings of how God had worked on behalf of His people (4:6). (3) It was to teach the Israelite children of God's power (cf. vv. 22–24). (4) It was to teach the nations of the earth that the Lord alone is God (v. 24).

This was not an unusual procedure, for Scripture contains incidents where Israel used similar methods of teaching their children: (1) The Feast of the Passover was a teaching device for the children to show them God had redeemed the nation Israel from out of Egypt by the applied blood (Exod. 12:26–27). (2) The firstborn animals of the Israelites were the Lord's and were set apart for Him (13:12–14). (3) The law was a sign of how God wanted the nation to live after He brought them up out of Egypt (Deut. 6:20–25).

B. Placing of the Memorial Stones in the Jordan (4:8–18)

These verses indicate there were two memorials. The first was at Gilgal, on the land, to show *what* happened (4:8; cf. v. 19f.). The second memorial was in the river to show *where* it happened (vv. 9–18). The question would arise whether this second memorial served any real purpose. After all, wouldn't these stones be quickly washed away by the flow of the river? Keil and Delitzsch respond:

> The monument did not fail of its object, even if it only existed a short time. The account of its erection, which was handed down by tradition, would necessarily help to preserve the remembrance of the miraculous occurrence. But it cannot be so absolutely affirmed that these stones would be carried away at once by the stream, so that they could never be seen any more. As the priests did not stand in the middle or deepest part of the river, but just in the bed of the river, and close to its eastern bank, and it was upon this spot that the stones were set up, and as we neither know their size nor the firmness with which they stood, we cannot pronounce any positive opinion as to the possibility of their remaining.[1]

The priests had stationed themselves in the riverbed while the people hurried across (4:10). The quiet calmness of the priests contrasts with the hurried activity of the people. Why did the people hurry? Possibly it was out of consideration for the priests, who had to remain standing until more than two million people had crossed over! Another possible reason for the haste was fear.

---

[1]Keil and Delitzsch, *Joshua, Judges, Ruth*, p. 49.

When all the people had crossed over, the priests with the ark left their station in the middle of the Jordan, crossed over themselves, and came again to the front of the procession. The ark of the Lord is mentioned ahead of the priests to denote its importance, and God's presence in the ark provided the miracle on behalf of the nation.

The account of Reuben, Gad, and the half-tribe of Manasseh is a supplementary statement, indicating that these tribes that had already decided to settle on the eastern side of the Jordan River were joining the other tribes on the western side to conquer the land according to the command of Moses (4:12–13; Num. 32:20–32). Since only 40,000 are mentioned as going forth to battle alongside their brothers, the majority of the two and a half tribes remained on the eastern side of the Jordan—probably to protect and provide for the women and children (see comments on 1:12–15). According to the new census, Reuben numbered 43,730 men twenty years old and upward (Num. 26:7); Gad numbered 40,500 (Num. 26:18), and the half-tribe of Manasseh numbered 26,350 (Num. 26:34). The military purpose of the 40,000 is emphasized by the terms, "armed," "armed for battle," and "crossed over . . . for war" (4:12–13).

The repeated promises of the Lord that He would be with Joshua just as He had been with Moses were initially fulfilled in 4:14 as the Lord exalted Joshua in the sight of all the people. This promise originally had been given in 3:7 and was now fulfilled at the crossing of the Jordan. The people recognized the parallel of God's exalting Moses at the crossing of the Red Sea and of God's exalting Joshua at the crossing of the Jordan River. The result was that the people revered Joshua just as they had revered Moses. The Hebrew word for "revere" means to "fear, honor or reverence"; it is used in regard to honoring parents (Lev. 19:3) and honoring the commandments of God (Prov. 13:13), but particularly of reverencing God (Exod. 18:21; Deut. 28:58). The Israelites recognized Joshua as their mediator before God.

After all the people had crossed the riverbed of Jordan, the priests also came up from where they were standing. As soon as their feet touched the dry ground above the riverbed, the water resumed its flow as before, indicating once more the miraculous nature of the event (4:18).

C. Placing of the Memorial Stones at Gilgal (4:19–5:1)

God's timing for His people was exactly right. They entered the land "on the tenth day of the first month" (4:19). The time was significant for Nisan was the first month in the Hebrew calendar and the month in which God had commanded the Jews to celebrate the Passover. In fact, it was on this very day (10th of Nisan) that Israel was to select the animal to celebrate the Passover in commemorating their deliverance from bondage in Egypt (Exod. 12:2–3). By having Israel enter the land on this very day, the Lord was reminding them of His faithfulness in delivering them from bondage and bringing them into the Promised Land. It was now exactly forty years since they had left Egypt (Deut. 1:3).

After the memorial stones were placed at Gilgal (4:20), Joshua explained the significance of the memorial to the people: (1) The memorial was to teach their children and generations to follow what the Lord had done on their behalf (vv. 21–22). The miracle of the Jordan crossing was to be associated with the miracle at the Red Sea (v. 23). That Israel heeded the injunction to perpetuate these historic miracles is seen in later writings. Psalm 66:6 refers to both the Red Sea crossing and the Jordan crossing in ascribing praise to God (cf. 106:9 and 114:3 where reference is again made to both events). (2) The memorial was to remind the nations of the world of the power of the Lord (Josh. 4:24). The news of the Lord's awesome power in bringing Israel into the land would aid Israel in her conquest of the land.

The miracle had the effect of deflating the courage and fighting morale of the inhabitants of the land. "Their hearts sank and they no longer had the courage to face the Israelites" (5:1). They were in a state of panic. The word "heart" denotes the "will, the inner man, the mind"; here it specifically refers to "the seat of the emotions" in turmoil, for the inhabitants were awestruck by the miracle.

The inhabitants of the land are described by two general categories, the Amorites and the Canaanites. The Amorites are representative of all the inhabitants who lived in the central hill country, while the Canaanites designate the people living along the Mediterranean seacoast.

For Further Study

1. Read an article on memorials in a Bible dictionary or encyclopedia.

2. Find other examples of memorials in Scripture and study their significance.

3. What does it mean to fear or reverence the Lord? How is this attitude toward God expressed?

Chapter 5

Consecration of the People
(Joshua 5:2–15)

The Lord had brought Israel to the threshold of the land. He had promised them success when they engaged in war against their enemies, but their success was conditioned on their adherence to the law (1:5–8). During the desert wanderings Israel had failed, neglecting many of the Lord's commands. To remedy the situation and to ensure success, Joshua performed the rite of circumcision on the generation that had been born in the desert.

A. The New Position: Circumcision (5:2–9)

"At that time" links the present narrative with the preceding portion. The Amorites and Canaanites were filled with fear when Joshua carried out the ritual of circumcision. It was an opportune moment for Israel to carry out the ritual without fear of invasion by their enemies.

The rite of circumcision was an important ritual for it was a sign to the Jewish males that God had ratified the Abrahamic covenant, promising a land, a seed, and a blessing to the nation Israel (Gen. 17:10–14). Normally, every male child was circumcised at the age of eight days (v. 12); however, this rite had been neglected during the forty years of desert wandering. The males born after the departure from Egypt had not been circumcised, and hence all males under forty submitted to the rite. By being circumcised, these men placed themselves under the covenant. It was an act of faith that anticipated the blessing of God in the land.

Joshua made flint knives with which to circumcise those who had not previously been circumcised. The word "again" in 5:2, of course, does not refer to a second ritual on the same males, but rather means the ritual was now being done as it had formerly been practiced. That which had been neglected was now to be performed as it had been previously practiced. Flint knives may have been used because of tradition (cf. Exod. 4:25), since bronze tools had replaced stone tools by this time. The location of the ritual was later known as Gibeath-haaraloth, meaning "hill of foreskins."

In verses 4f. the explanation for the circumcision is given. All the men who came out of Egypt had been circumcised, but that generation of men, from twenty years old and upward, perished in the desert because of disobedience (Num. 14:29) and thus did not enter the land. However, the new generation of men who was replacing the rebels had not been circumcised (5:5). They needed this mark in the flesh before God could bring them into the land and bless them.

The newly circumcised men remained at Gilgal until they were healed (5:7–8). As a result of the Israelites' obedience to the covenant of Abraham signified in circumcision, God told Joshua that the "reproach of Egypt" had been rolled away from them (5:9). Two basic thoughts are involved in the phrase "reproach of Egypt." (1) God had withheld His covenant blessings from the generation of rebels that died in the desert.[1] (2) The Egyptians derided Israel, suggesting God had taken them into the desert in order to slay them (Exod. 32:12). When the Israelites obeyed the command to be circumcised, God removed from them the reproach of Egypt. The people again stood under the blessing of God, who promised to give them the land as their inheritance. In recognition of this significant event, the place was named Gilgal, meaning "rolling," to signify that God rolled away the reproach of Egypt from Israel there.

B. The New Beginning: Passover (5:10)

Four days after entering the land (cf. 4:19), the Israelites observed the Feast of the Passover. Although forty years had passed since the Passover had been instituted (Exod. 12:1–14), yet this was only the third recorded time in the history of the nation that the Passover had been kept. They had observed it on the first anniversary of their departure from Egypt (Num. 9:1–14), but the memorial was probably suspended following Israel's failure at Kadesh Barnea (Num. 14). The

---

[1]As Keil and Delitzsch point out, this was not a dissolution of the covenant relationship with the nation as a whole, but only the abrogation of the covenant with that particular generation. Cf. Keil and Delitzsch, *Joshua, Judges, Ruth*, pp. 54–58. Cf. also Rea, "Joshua," p. 211.

Passover was intended to be an annual feast, a reminder to the nation Israel of their redemption out of Egypt (cf. Lev. 23:6). It was to be kept continually as a memorial (Exod. 12:14).

C. The New Food: Produce of the Land (5:11–12)

Deuteronomy 28 relates the principle by which God worked with Israel: obedience brings blessing; disobedience brings chastisement. That principle is operative in 5:11–12. Following Israel's obedience in practicing circumcision and in keeping the memorial of Passover, God blessed the nation by giving them the firstfruits of the land. On the next day following the Passover, Israel ate some of the produce of the land. This was God's "down payment" to Israel, indicating He was giving them the land.

On the next day the manna, which they had eaten for forty years, ceased (cf. Exod. 16:35). Manna was God's food provision when Israel was en route to the Promised Land; now that they were entering the land, they would be sustained by this land God had given them. The first meal from the Promised Land consisted of unleavened bread and roasted grain. The latter would have been new grain, taken from that year's harvest. The grain was roasted in a pan and eaten along with the unleavened bread. The Israelites would have followed the prescribed ritual prior to eating the firstfruits (Lev. 23:5–14). The writer does not mention this, for a knowledge of the law is assumed.

D. The New Captain: The Lord (5:13–15)

Joshua had come to Jericho and was considering the conquest of the city when he was confronted by a man with a drawn sword in his hand. After Joshua queried whether he was a friend or foe, the man responded, "Neither, but as commander of the army of the LORD I have now come." "Commander" signifies a military leader, a general. It is the same term used in the phrase "Prince of Peace" in Isaiah 9:6. This man had come as commander of the "army of the LORD." The expression indicates this commander was not the military leader of a mere earthly realm, but of the host of heaven. He was the commander of God's angelic army. The concept is similar to that presented in 1 Kings 22:19 where the prophet Micaiah saw the "host of heaven" attending the Lord, who was seated on His throne. The expression "army of the LORD" in 5:14 thus designates the angels of heaven (cf. Pss. 103:21; 148:2), but more particularly in warfare for the Lord.

When Joshua heard the response, he fell on his face and worshiped to show that he understood the identity of the One before him. While bowing down before a guest was a common Oriental custom, it appears that in 5:14 the act goes beyond the simple formality and points to Joshua's recognition of the man as the Angel of the Lord.

The appearance of the man is best understood as a theophany, a manifestation of Christ in the Old Testament. A theophany usually took the form of an angel or a man and is most frequently designated in the Old Testament as "The Angel of the Lord"[2] (cf. Gen. 16:7–13; 21:17; 22:11–18; 24:7, 40; 31:11; 32:24–32; 48:15–16; Exod. 3:2; Judg. 6:11–24; 13:3–23 et al.).

The fact that the commander had his sword drawn is noteworthy: it pointed to the coming judgment on the inhabitants of the land. Thus 5:13–15 can be seen as the *basis* for the conquest of chapters 6–12. The theophany provides the transition from Israel's entrance into the land to Israel's conquest of the land. Although Joshua was Israel's human captain, the Lord Himself was now preparing to lead His people in battle against the enemy.

But 5:13–15 is important for an additional reason. There is a decided parallel between Moses' encounter with the Lord at the burning bush (Exod. 3) and Joshua's meeting with the commander of the army of the Lord. We see here a further verification of Joshua's position and authority as the legitimate successor to Moses. Even as the Lord had called and commissioned Moses, so He was now placing His approval on Moses' successor. That this analogy is evident is seen in 5:15: "Take off your sandals, for the place where you are standing is holy" (cf. Exod. 3:5). Just as it was made clear to Moses that he was in the presence of the Lord, so Joshua came to the same realization. Amid a land defiled by an idolatrous people, the place where the Lord stood was holy— sanctified because of His presence.

Joshua acknowledged the Lord's leadership, as we learn in the concluding statement of 5:15; he submitted to the Lord's leadership in battle. The Lord had earlier delineated the reasons why Israel was going to be given the land and why He would drive out the inhabitants: "on account of the wickedness of these nations, the LORD your God will drive them out before you" (Deut. 9:5). The nations dwelling in the

---

[2]For further discussions of Old Testament theophanies, see J. Barton Payne, *The Theology of the Older Testament* (Grand Rapids: Zondervan, 1962), pp. 45–47, 167–170; John F. Walvoord, *Jesus Christ Our Lord* (Chicago: Moody Press, 1969), pp. 51–55.

land were corrupt and immoral; the Lord wanted to preserve Israel from contamination by the heathen; hence He would drive them out (18:9-14). The stage was now set for the conquest mentioned in Joshua 6-12.

For Further Study

1. In a bible dictionary or encyclopedia, read the articles on circumcision, Passover, and theophany.

2. What is the relationship of obedience to success and disobedience to failure?

3. Reflect on how God has worked in your life in the past. Can you see how He has worked in different ways for different events and circumstances?

4. Search the Bible for passages that promise victory to the believer (e.g., 2 Cor. 2:14). Commit them to memory.

PART TWO: SUBJECTION OF THE LAND

Chapter 6

The Central Campaign
(Joshua 6:1–8:29)

The strategy for the conquest of Canaan involved three phases: the central campaign, the southern campaign, and the northern campaign. It was a strategic maneuver since it nullified, for the most part, any significant union of the city-states in opposing Israel.

A. Jericho (6:1–27)

The invasion of Jericho was important because of the city's strategic location. Here, nomadic tribes entered the land through several valleys leading from the city to the central ridge of the land. Furthermore, by entering the land at Jericho, Israel could divide the land in two, prohibiting any significant alliances between the northern city-states and the southern inhabitants. This strategic plan can be seen as divine guidance by the commander of the Lord's army.

1. Instruction for battle (6:1–5)

The opening statement of chapter 6 reveals Jericho as "tightly shut" because of the Israelites, with no one entering or leaving. This is an explanatory clause actually interrupting the conversation between the Lord and Joshua. It shows that the city of Jericho was tightly sealed off and fortified against any invasion, and it also depicts the fear of the people of Jericho.

From a human standpoint, the conquest of Jericho was impossible. The Lord had previously indicated He would lead them in battle (Deut. 9:1–6; 12:29; 18:9–14; Josh. 5:13–15), and that now became essential if Jericho was to be conquered. Jericho's defense was formidable.

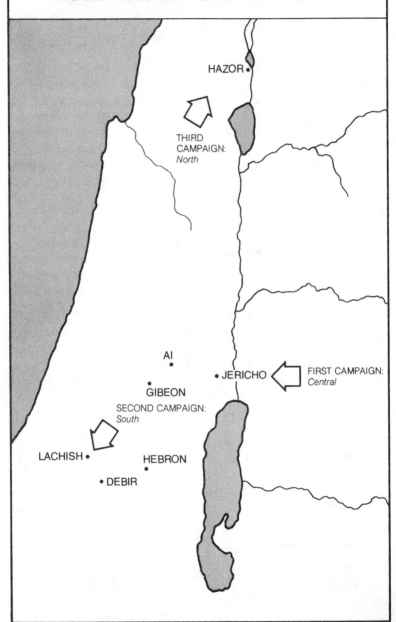

THE THREE CAMPAIGNS

HAZOR •

THIRD
CAMPAIGN:
North

AI
•

• JERICHO

FIRST CAMPAIGN:
Central

•
GIBEON

SECOND CAMPAIGN:
South

LACHISH •

HEBRON
•

• DEBIR

The walls were of a type which made direct assault practically impossible. An approaching enemy first encountered a stone abutment, eleven feet high, back and up from which sloped a thirty-five degree plastered scarp reaching to the main wall some thirty-five vertical feet above. The steep smooth slope prohibited battering the wall by any effective device or building fires to break it. An army trying to storm the wall found difficulty in climbing the slope, and ladders to scale it could find no satisfactory footing. The normal tactic used by an enemy to take a city so protected was seige, but Israel did not have time for this, if she was to occupy all the land in any reasonable number of months.[1]

It is possible that the scarp existed only at the approach to the city. But in addition the defenses included a fortification of two walls that surrounded the city; the outer wall was six feet thick and the inner wall twelve feet thick. The city was built on a mound, making the invasion even more difficult. Unger describes the wall structure further:

A massive six-foot-thick wall was erected on the edge of the mound. The inner wall was separated from it by a space of from twelve to fifteen feet, and was itself twelve feet thick. The wall originally reached perhaps a height of about thirty feet. . . . The crowded condition led to the erection of houses over the space between the inner and outer walls.[2]

Joshua 6:2 continues the conversation between the commander and Joshua. We notice that while He is referred to as "commander of the army of the LORD" in 5:14, in 6:2 He is designated "the LORD." The commander of the Lord's army was promising Joshua the down payment of Israel's appropriation of the land. God was giving them the city; it would not be taken by the ingenuity of men, but by the power of God.

In 6:3-5 the Lord explained to Joshua precisely how Israel would capture the city. It was surely unorthodox! For six days, once a day, all the warring men of Israel were to march around Jericho without giving a war cry. Seven priests blowing seven trumpets were to precede the ark.

It seems to have a religio-ceremonial significance, announcing the arrival of Jehovah as King, whether to his people to complete his covenant or proclaim release and liberty, or to his enemies to judge and smite them.[3]

On the seventh day the people would march around the city seven times instead of just once. The seven priests before the ark would blow

---

[1]Wood, *Survey of Israel's History*, p. 174.

[2]Unger, *Archaeology and the Old Testament*, p. 147. For a detailed discussion, complete with plates, see John Garstang, *Joshua-Judges* (Grand Rapids: Kregel, 1978 reprint), pp. 140-148, 386-388; Kathleen M. Kenyon, *Archaeology in the Holy Land* (New York: Frederick A. Praeger, 1960), pp. 176f.; Kathleen M. Kenyon, *Digging Up Jericho* (New York: Frederick A. Praeger, 1957).

[3]Rea, *Joshua*, p. 212.

their seven trumpets. The emphasis on seven is obvious and seems to point to the "completeness" of the event.[4] The trumpets used by the priests were curved ram's horns called shofars; these horns produced loud, far-reaching tones. The shofar was important in the religious life of Israel as it was sounded each Friday evening to announce the beginning of the Sabbath. It was also sounded in proclaiming the Feast of Trumpets (Lev. 23:24) that has great prophetic significance (Isa. 27:13; Joel 2:1f.). The sound of the trumpets in Joshua 6 was the announcement of blessing in the land which the Lord their God was giving them.

When the city had been circled seven times and when the priests had blown their trumpets, the people were to break their silence and shout with a great shout. The city wall would fall down flat in its place—a reminder that the Lord had accomplished it. To prevent confusion, the Israelites were to "go up, every man straight in" (6:5).

2. *Organization for battle* (6:6–11)

a) *The priests* (6:6–8)

While this was a strange battle plan, there is no indication that Joshua doubted the word of the Lord. He summoned the priests according to the Lord's command and instructed seven of them to march before the ark, each one with a ram's horn (6:6). The priests and the ark formed the center of the march; leading the procession were the armed men (v. 7). The rear guard followed the priests (v. 9), while some of the people made up the retinue. In the Hebrew text the pronoun "he" of verse 7 is "they," indicating Joshua himself did not give the commands but gave them through his appointed officers (cf. 1:10–11).

Having been commanded by Joshua through the officers, the entire procession began. It was a curious occasion and there is no record concerning a response by the people of Jericho. It may have been one of ridicule,[5] or fear.[6] In any case, the Israelites responded in faith to the strange command. They trusted the Lord as their King.

b) *The armed men* (6:9)

Two groups of soldiers are mentioned: the armed guard going before

---

[4]The study of numerology in Scripture must be approached with caution since excesses result in the absurd as pointed out by O. T. Allis, *Bible Numerics* (Philadelphia: Presbyterian and Reformed Publishing Co., 1974). For a balanced and helpful approach, consult Davis, *Biblical Numerology*.

[5]William Garden Blaikie, *The Book of Joshua* (Minneapolis: Klock & Klock Christian Publishers, 1978 reprint), p. 137.

[6]Davis, *Conquest and Crisis*, p. 43.

the priests and the rear guard that followed. The former group probably refers to the fighting men of the eastern tribes (4:13), while the latter refers to the fighting men from the other tribes.

c) *Joshua* (6:10–11)

Amid solemn silence the entire procession marches around the city—silent except for the continual, eerie blasts from the trumpets and the shuffle of feet. The people were to keep silent until commanded by Joshua to "shout." Having circled the city once, the procession returned to camp (6:11).

3. *Procession around the city* (6:12–14)

The procession continued to march around the city, once a day for six days. Still no sound was heard—except the continual blowing of the trumpets. The text emphasizes the use of the trumpets (6:13).

> The constant blowing of the ceremonial trumpets served not only to remind the Israelites of the spiritual nature of their conflict but also to strike terror into the hearts of their adversaries; the awesome sound, persisting day after day, must have suggested supernatural power.[7]

4. *Destruction of the city* (6:15–21)

a) *The march* (6:15)

At the dawning of the seventh day, the Israelites arose and proceeded to march around Jericho as before. The early rising was necessary because on this day they would march around the city seven times.

b) *The shout* (6:16–19)

When the contingent had marched around the city for the seventh time, Joshua commanded, "Shout! For the Lord has given you the city!" (6:16). Along with the command, Joshua issued the warning that the city was "to be devoted" (v. 17, "under the ban," NASB). This meant everything in the city belonged to the Lord; therefore, the Israelites were prohibited from taking any spoils for themselves.

The term "devoted" is of considerable consequence to the discussion. The underlying Hebrew word *herem* is equivalent to the Greek word *"anathema"* and most often means "devoting to destruction cities of Canaanites and other neighbours of Isr., *exterminating* inhabitants, and destroying or appropriating their possessions."[8]

---

[7]Blair, "Joshua," p. 240.
[8]Francis Brown, S. R. Driver, and C. A. Briggs, *A Hebrew and English Lexicon of the Old Testament* (Oxford: Clarendon Press, 1968), p. 355.

Several important conclusions concerning the term "devoted" can be made: (1) The inhabitants of Jericho were devoted to God for destruction, that is, they were to be put to death. The use of *herem* in Exodus 22:20 clarifies this as "must be destroyed," referring to capital punishment. In Leviticus 27:29 *herem* also emphasizes the irrevocable nature of the command. (2) Israel's idolatrous enemies were devoted to destruction, according to Deuteronomy 20:17–18. Verse 18 indicates that the Canaanites were to be destroyed because their idolatry jeopardized Israel's faith in the Lord. The idolaters could lead Israel away from worshiping the Lord. (3) While people could be irrevocably devoted to destruction, material goods were sometimes devoted to the Lord for sacred use (Num. 18:14; Ezek. 44:29). In Jericho the silver, gold, bronze, and iron were to be set apart for the treasury of the Lord (6:19). This is also seen in the fact that Israel, prior to the destruction of Jericho, was permitted to take spoils (Deut. 2:35), and afterward they also took spoils (Josh. 8:27; 11:14). (4) The prohibition concerning the spoils at Jericho was given because Jericho in its entirety was devoted to the Lord as the firstfruits of the land; hence the city served as a sign that the Israelites would receive all Canaan from Him.[9]

Only Rahab and her household were excluded from being "devoted" for destruction (6:16). All within her house would be spared (v. 17). The reason is that Rahab acted in faith and submission to the Lord when she hid the spies; that act signified her repudiation of idolatry and her trust in Israel's God. For that reason she and all who came into her house would live.

Conversely, any Israelite who would take something devoted for destruction would himself be destroyed (6:18). By taking of the spoils he identified himself with that which was devoted to destruction. Verse 18 anticipates the sin of Achan in chapter 7 and explains the reason for his death and that of his family. By partaking of that which was devoted to destruction, this family thereby brought about their own destruction.

c) *The collapse* (6:20)

Upon completing the seventh circuit, Joshua gave the signal and the people shouted their battle cry. The walls immediately fell down, opening Jericho to invasion. Garstang describes the destruction:

> The main defences of Jericho in the Late Bronze Age (c. 1600–1200 B.C.) followed the upper brink of the city mound, and comprised two parallel

[9]Davis, *Conquest and Crisis*, p. 46.

walls, the outer six feet and the inner twelve feet thick. Investigations along the west side show continuous signs of destruction and conflagration. The outer wall suffered most, its remains falling down the slope. The inner wall is preserved only where it abuts upon the citadel, or tower, to a height of eighteen feet; elsewhere it is found largely to have fallen, together with the remains of buildings upon it, into the space between the walls which was filled with ruins and debris. Traces of intense fire are plain to see, including reddened masses of brick, cracked stones, charred timbers and ashes. Houses alongside the wall are found burned to the ground, their roofs fallen upon the domestic pottery within.[10]

Was the collapse of the walls due to a natural phenomenon or was it caused by a miracle? Some writers suggest the cause was an earthquake; however, the text indicates the walls fell at precisely the moment that the people shouted, and this rules out the view that an earthquake occurred at precisely that moment. Moreover, there is no indication in the text of an earthquake. It is better to understand the event as the second in a series of miracles in which the Lord worked on behalf of His people. It was a second demonstration by the Lord that He was giving Israel the land. Upon Israel's approach to the land the flooded Jordan parted; upon Israel's entrance into the land, Jericho's walls collapsed. Each was a visible demonstration that the land was Israel's inheritance. God was faithfully keeping His promise to give Israel the land.

d) *The ruin* (6:21)

Upon entering the city, the Israelites obeyed the injunction of the Lord to destroy everything. *Herem*, the Hebrew word for "devoted" that occurs in 6:17, now reoccurs in verse 21. According to the command that had been given them, Israel devoted the entire city with all living things to the Lord for destruction.

5. *Salvation of Rahab* (6:22–25)

The two spies who had gone to Rahab's house originally were now sent by Joshua to rescue Rahab and her relatives from her house. Although Rahab's house was built on the wall (2:15), her house remained intact. Perhaps that immediate section of the wall did not

---

[10]Garstang, *Joshua–Judges*, pp. 145–146. The point of the discussion is not whether Garstang was right or wrong concerning his "double wall" theory, but to indicate the enormity of the destruction when the wall(s) collapsed. If the walls Garstang identified as City IV were actually earlier, it is possible the Canaanites of Joshua's day reused the older walls in reoccupying the site (cf. Davis, *Conquest and Crisis*, pp. 47–48).

collapse. The Lord may have preserved Rahab's house by performing a miracle similar to the one He performed in sparing Israel in Goshen. While the hail rained down on the Egyptians, the land of Goshen where Israel lived was spared (Exod. 9:26). Similarly, Rahab's house may have been spared although there was destruction all around.

The two Israelites brought Rahab, her parents, and her brothers out of her house. The statement "and all who belonged to her" (6:23) refers to other immediate relatives, including those by birth or marriage. They were placed outside the camp of Israel for cleansing from their idolatries (perhaps for seven days according to the purification law of Num. 31:19), for the rite of circumcision, and for their introduction into the Hebrew faith.

After Rahab and her family were removed from the city and the other inhabitants and all their domestic animals had been killed, the city was set on fire. Only the valuable metals were spared and put in the treasury of the Lord.[11]

Rahab and her family were spared and probably adopted the faith of Israel. The statement "and she lives among the Israelites to this day" (6:25) is interesting, for it points to a date of writing of these events not long after they occurred. That Rahab integrated into Hebrew society, experiencing the grace of God, is further seen in the genealogy of Jesus Christ where she is listed as an ancestor of the Messiah (Matt. 1:5).

6. *Declaration against the city* (6:26–27)

The curse on the city of Jericho also had future repercussions, as Joshua announced the curse on the man who would rise up and rebuild the city. The result of the judgment would be the loss of his firstborn son as well as his youngest son. It is possible that the curse on Jericho

---

[11]Whether Israel was justified in the complete slaughter of the Canaanites is an important moral question. John Davis provides an excellent summary of the issues involved: "First of all, it should be noted that the destruction of Canaanite cities was based on religious, not political or military considerations (Deut. 7:2–6; 12:2–3; 20:10–18). Secondly, the action taken at Jericho (and also at Ai) was done on the basis of *divine command* (Deut. 7:2; Josh. 8:2; Exod. 17:14; Deut. 20:16) and thus involves the moral character of God. If we believe that God is holy and without imperfection, it follows that whatever He commands will be just and right. And, thirdly, it was really *Jehovah* who was destroying these cities and their peoples (Josh. 6:2; 24:8). Israel should merely be regarded as God's instruments of destruction. Fourthly, the *reason* for this command is clearly stated in Scripture and seems to justify the action taken. For example, Deuteronomy 20:18 makes it clear that this demand was designed to preserve the religious purity of the nation of Israel. The destruction of various Canaanite cities should be regarded as a direct judgment from God because of their iniquity (Gen. 15:16–21, cf. Gen. 19)," Davis, *Conquest and Crisis*, p. 49.

was illustrated by the Israelites spreading salt over the area to symbolize the curse and to depict the continuing barrenness (Judg. 9:45).

The curse itself, however, did not relate simply to the rebuilding of the city, for it appears the city was rebuilt without incident (Josh. 18:21; Judg. 3:13; 2 Sam. 10:5). The term "rebuild" in 6:26 refers to the refortification of the city and its use as a military base. The underlying Hebrew term is so used in 1 Kings 15:17 and 2 Chronicles 11:5. The prophecy of the curse was fulfilled in 1 Kings 16:34 when Hiel of Bethel refortified Jericho and his firstborn son, Abiram, and his youngest son, Segub, both died as a result.

The conclusion to chapter 6 indicates the Lord was fulfilling His promise to Joshua (cf. 1:5). Joshua had acceded to the leadership of Israel as Moses' legitimate successor and was recognized by all the people. The chapter closes with a summary statement of the two great miracles through which Joshua had been magnified before the people (6:27).

B. Ai (7:1–8:29)

The Israelites moved westward in their pursuit to conquer the land. The next conflict would involve Ai, located about two miles east of Bethel on the eastern side of the central ridge that runs through Palestine. Ai lay on a major trade route running north and south, through Jerusalem, Beersheba, and on to Egypt.

A problem exists concerning the interpretation of archaeological data with respect to Ai. While conservative scholars hold to an early date for the invasion of the land (i.e., 1406 B.C.), archaeological data has apparently indicated there was an occupational gap at Ai between c. 2200 B.C. until after 1200 B.C. Madame Judith Marquet-Krause, who excavated the site from 1933 to 1935, discovered that Ai had been a flourishing city during the third millennium B.C., but had been destroyed c. 2200 B.C. and had remained unoccupied for one thousand years.

It is difficult to dogmatize concerning a solution, but there are several possibilities: (1) The narrative concerning the destruction of Ai really refers to Bethel, a view held by William F. Albright. This view is also suggested because there is no specific account of Bethel's capture. The major problem with this view is that it conflicts with the biblical narrative, which clearly distinguishes between Ai and Bethel (cf. 8:12). (2) The identification of Ai is incorrect. Et-tell, the suggested location of Ai, is actually another city and Ai remains unidentified.[12] (3) Ai was only a temporary military outpost of Bethel and was used to check the advance of military expeditions against Bethel. This view has been proposed by Hugues Vincent, who suggested the outpost was of such modest proportions that it left no remains for the archaeologist. A problem with this view is that the text indicates Ai had a king (8:29; 12:9)—unlikely if Ai was only an outpost. (4) Future excavations may provide more information that will provide a further understanding of the problem.

1. *Defeat at Ai* (7:1–26)

Joshua is the book of success, recounting the Lord's faithfulness in bringing Israel into the land. Joshua 7 is an exception to the general theme of the book, as it records the failure of Israel due to the sin of Achan.

a) *Disobedience of Achan* (7:1)

The statement of 7:1 sets the stage for the defeat that followed and points the reader to the reason for the defeat; namely, Achan's sin. Achan, of the tribe of Judah, took some of the forbidden things and thus incurred the anger of God (see comments on 6:16–19). In effect, Achan stole from God, for all the items in the city were dedicated to God either in destruction or for the treasury of the Lord. This is substantiated by 6:17: "The city and all that is in it are to be devoted to the LORD."

By taking some of the devoted things, Achan brought destruction on himself and the threat of destruction on the nation Israel. God viewed the entire nation as responsible, imputing the crime of Achan to all the people. One man sinned; the whole nation suffered. The concept of imputation is a principle of Scripture concerning sin for the entire human race (through Adam) and concerning righteousness for those who believe (through Christ) (cf. Rom. 5:12–21).

---

[12]Kenneth Kitchen states, "Excavations at Et-Tell have failed to produce any proper evidence of occupation there after the Early Bronze Age (*c.* 2400 BC), apart from a small Israelite settlement (Iron I) of *c.* 1200–1050 BC. Despite assertions sometimes made to the contrary, this situation suggests that Et-Tell is *not* Ai but another ancient site (Beth-Aven?), and that Ai must be looked for somewhere else in the area and not on Et-Tell" (K. A. Kitchen, *Ancient Orient and Old Testament;* Chicago: Inter-Varsity Press, 1966), p. 63. Leon Wood also leans toward this view and adds, "Et-Tell (the suggested location of Ai) is rather far from Bethel whereas Joshua 12:9 (cf. 7:2) states that Ai was 'beside *(mitsad)* Bethel'; also Et-Tell is a comparatively large mound whereas Joshua's reconnaissance party described Ai's inhabitants as few," Wood, *A Survey of Israel's History,* p. 176.

b) *Defeat of Israel* (7:2-5)

As in the case of Jericho, Joshua sent spies to Ai to learn about the enemy. Ai was near Beth Aven, east of Bethel about two miles. Beth Aven, which means "house of iniquity," is unknown. The name is in contrast to Bethel, which means "house of God." Later Beth Aven came to be used as a synonym for apostate Bethel (Hos. 10:5).

When the spies returned, they gave their report: send only about 2,000 or 3,000 men. This evaluation would agree with the statement in 8:25 that indicates a population of 12,000 inhabitants. A realistic figure of fighting men would probably be 3,000 men; hence, the spies suggested Israel would need only 2,000 or 3,000 men to take Ai. An important reason for taking only a few men to fight against Ai is given in the statement "do not weary all the people" (7:3). Although the march from Gilgal westward to Bethel represented only about 15 miles of travel, it was a difficult one. Gilgal was 900 feet below sea level, while Ai was about 2,600 feet above sea level; so the march was a tedious uphill trek.

The Israelites were stunned by what followed. When the approximately 3,000 Israelites approached Ai, the men of Ai rose up against them and slew 36 Israelites. The Israelites fled from the city. Their enemies pursued them downhill as far as the stone quarries that were rugged, broken fissures in the land. The result was that the hearts of the people melted and became as water—their response was now similar to that of the heathen (2:10-11; 5:1).

c) *Dismay of Joshua* (7:6-9)

When Joshua heard the news, he tore his clothes and he and the elders put dust on their heads. Both the tearing of clothes and the putting of dust on the head were symbols of extreme grief, mourning, and humiliation. This procedure was carried out for varying reasons: at the death of a person (1 Sam. 4:12), at extreme illness (Job. 2:12), or because of blasphemy (Acts 14:14).

Joshua was upset to the point that his complaint sounded like the murmuring of the Israelites in the desert (cf. Num. 14:2-3). In the light of present circumstances, the Israelites thought it better not to have crossed the Jordan into Canaan. The prayer of Joshua reflects both the negative and positive thoughts. Perhaps this turmoil that Joshua displays indicates that he is unaware of the cause of the defeat. Perhaps, therefore, the negative statement of 7:7 should be seen as the struggle amid his confused thoughts. The statement is certainly subordinate to what follows, where the focus is on God's honor (vv. 8–9). Jamieson states,

> Although apparently breathing a spirit of bold remonstrance and complaint, it was in reality the effusion of a deeply-humbled and afflicted mind, expressing his belief that God could not, after having so miraculously brought His people over Jordan into the promised land, intend to destroy them, to expose them to the insults of their triumphant enemies, and bring reproach upon His own name for inconstancy or unkindness to His people, or inability to resist their enemies.[13]

Joshua's ultimate concern is stated in 7:9: "What then will you do for your own great name?" While Joshua acknowledged the possibility of Israel's extermination, his greater concern was for God's honor. What was God going to do to preserve His great name now that this tragedy had occurred? The thought is reminiscent of occasions when Moses feared that in the ridicule of the Israelites the other nations would say that the Lord had been unable to bring His people into the land and therefore slaughtered them in the desert (cf. Num. 14:15–16; Deut. 9:28).

d) *Direction of the Lord* (7:10–15)

The Lord's anger against Israel is clearly seen in His words of rebuke to Joshua: "Stand up! What are you doing down on your face?" (7:10). Joshua was looking for the answer in the wrong place. Instead of questioning the faithfulness of God, he ought to have been looking for the sin among the people. The commands "stand up!" and "Go" (vv. 10, 13) constitute a rebuke and a reminder that from this point on Joshua is to deal with the dilemma. That Joshua was to seek the solution to the failure among the people is seen in the explicit statement "Israel has sinned" (v. 11).

In elaborating on Israel's sin, the Lord said this was a sin against Him; Israel had broken their covenant obligation (7:11; cf. Exod. 19:8). They had stolen devoted things that did not belong to them and they put the stolen items "with their own possessions," as though these things were their own. This was a "deliberate sin, which is violation of the covenant obligations solemnly laid upon Israel with adjurations."[14] This was the reason for Israel's failure (cf. Isa. 59:1–2). By taking the things devoted to God, they had made themselves liable to destruc-

---

[13]Robert Jamieson, "Joshua," *A Commentary Critical, Experimental, and Practical on the Old and New Testaments* (Grand Rapids: William B. Eerdmans Publishing Co., 1945 reprint), p. 18.
[14]Gray, *Joshua, Judges and Ruth*, p. 85.

tion; the nation was now subject to the curse of God rather than to His blessings. They would fail in every venture and in every battle unless they removed the accursed thing from among them.

The Lord commanded Joshua to gather the Israelites together to determine the guilty party. They were to consecrate themselves (cf. 3:5). The phrase "come forward" indicates the manner in which the guilty party would be discovered (7:14). It suggests they were to approach the sanctuary for divine arbitration[15] through the lot. There are several possibilities in identifying the lot: (1) It was the Urim and Thummim employed by the high priest (Exod. 28:30; Judg. 20:27–28). Two stones were kept in the ephod of the high priest. One stone signified yes, the other no. It is uncertain in what way the stones designated yes and no; possibly the yes stone was white and the no stone black. The high priest would reach into the pocket and pull out the stone; whatever the stone was, whether yes or no, that was the Lord's answer. (2) It is possible that little tablets or potsherds were used, with the names written on them; these were then drawn out of an urn.[16] Interestingly, Acts 1:26 represents the last occurrence of the lot in Scripture to determine God's will. With the descent of the Holy Spirit and the completion of the canon of Scripture, the lot became unnecessary. The sixty-six books of Scripture are adequate to guide Christian believers.

There was a fourfold narrowing process—through the tribe, the family, the household, and the man—in order to find the guilty person. First of all, the heads of the tribes would come forward to determine the tribe he belonged to; then the heads of the families of that particular tribe would come forward to discover the family; then the households within that family clan would come forward; finally, the individuals within the household that had been determined would come. In that manner the guilty person would be discovered.

Following the execution of the sinful person and all that belonged to him, his body was to be burned. Burning or cremation was not normative for Israel[17] but was commanded here to show the Lord's abhorrence for the crime that had been committed. It indicated an intensified punishment for a serious crime (cf. Lev. 20:14; 21:9).

---

[15]Gray, *Joshua, Judges and Ruth*, p. 86.

[16]Keil and Delitzsch, *Joshua, Judges, Ruth*, p. 80.

[17]For a provocative study on the believer's attitude toward cremation, see Loraine Boettner, *Immortality* (Philadelphia: Presbyterian and Reformed Publishing Co., 1958).

The sin of Achan is termed "a disgraceful thing" (7:15). The Hebrew term frequently denotes flagrant immorality (Gen. 34:7; Deut. 22:21; Judg. 19:23; 20:6; 2 Sam. 13:12), but also a foolish and selfish attitude (1 Sam. 25:25) or godless speech (Isa. 32:6). It is a technical term denoting flagrant sin. "The classical example of one *nabal* by name and nature is Nabal (1 Sam. 25:25), who could not govern his indignation by discretion. This lack of control or wilful failure to govern one's temper, desire, or whim is *nebalah* in the Old Testament. *Nebalah beyisrael* denotes indulgence of one's person, desires, or impulses in defiance of the standards and sanctions of the community."[18]

e) *Discovery of Achan* (7:16–21)

Through the lot the guilty party was discovered on the following day. On the first lot, the identification was narrowed to the tribe of Judah; on the second lot the family of Zerahites was identified; on the third lot the family of Zimri was indicated; on the fourth lot, Achan was identified as the guilty party.

With forceful words of exhortation Joshua commanded Achan to "give glory to the LORD" (7:19). This phrase "is a solemn formula of adjuration, by which a person was summoned to confess the truth before the face of God (cf. John ix. 24)."[19] In telling the truth, Achan would be giving praise to God. This is seen in the phrase "tell me what you have done," which is explanatory regarding "give the LORD" and "give him the praise." In calling for Achan's confession, however, Joshua does not suggest the abrogation of the punishment that was determined on Achan and his family.

Confronted with the evidence, Achan confessed. He recognized that his sin was, above all, a sin against God (7:20). David similarly confessed sin (Ps. 51:4). Achan's sin consisted in his having taken what belonged to the Lord. In confessing he spelled out the process of the temptation and the yielding: "I saw . . . I coveted . . . and took" (7:21). This was similar to the sin of Eve (Gen. 3:6) and the sin of David (2 Sam. 11:2–14). Sin enters into a person through sinful cravings, the lust of the eyes, and boasting of what one has and does (1 John 2:15).

Achan coveted and took a robe from Babylonia (7:21; Heb., Shinar, which is identified with Babylon in Gen. 10:10). The garment was beautiful, ornately constructed, and probably one used for cultic purposes. It was "covered with coloured figures, either of men or animals,

---

[18]Gray, *Joshua, Judges and Ruth*, p. 87.
[19]Keil and Delitzsch, *Joshua, Judges, Ruth*, p. 81.

sometimes woven, at other times worked with the needle."[20] In archaeological findings at Ras Shamra, mention is made of garments
trimmed with jewels, some valued at ten shekels of silver.[21] In addition, Achan stole 200 shekels of silver and a wedge of gold weighing 50
shekels. There were differing weights for the shekel in biblical times,
but the common shekel was approximately $2/5$ ounce. The wedge of
gold was about ten inches long by one inch wide and one inch thick.

Having stolen the items, Achan hid them in his tent. It appears that
Achan deposited the robe on top with the gold underneath it and the
silver on the bottom (7:21).

f) *Death of Achan* (7:22–26)

Before any action was taken, Joshua sent messengers to Achan's tent
to uncover the evidence. The robe, silver, and gold were found as
Achan had reported. The stolen items were brought to Joshua and laid
down "before the LORD" (7:23). The latter phrase probably signifies
that the items were brought to the tabernacle, since that was where the
lot was cast to discover the guilty party (see comments on 7:14). It
would also indicate that the items were being returned to the Lord—
the rightful Owner from whom they had been taken.

In the judgment of Achan and his family, "all the Israelites were
involved (7:23; cf. vv. 24–25). This was important. The sin of Achan
had corrupted the nation, and now the nation had to show its rejection
of the sin among them. Achan, his family, his animals, and all his
belongings were brought to the Valley of Achor to be stoned. Thus the
law of Deuteronomy 13:12–17 was brought to bear on Achan, the head
of the family, who had brought his entire family into sin. He primarily
was the guilty one, but the entire family was held responsible for the
crime, and it is possible that the family assisted Achan in hiding the
goods in the tent. The principle of an entire family suffering for the sin
of one man is not unusual (cf. Num. 16:31–33). In a family God sees the
man as a representative and so through one corrupt man an entire
family could be corrupted. Through a corrupt family, an entire nation
could be corrupted. Sin had to be rooted out to prevent its cancerous
spreading.

The place where Achan and his family were stoned to death was the
Valley of Achor, meaning "the valley of trouble." The designation indicated what it had been to Achan and to the nation: trouble. The action

---

[20]Ibid.
[21]Gray, *Joshua, Judges and Ruth*, p. 88.

of "all Israel" (7:24–25) participating in the stoning of Achan indicates their rejection of the sin in their midst and their willingness to deal with the sin through the removal of it. This would open the way to future blessing and victory.

The memorial stones served as a reminder of the tragic event in the history of the nation (7:26). In contrast to the stones at Gilgal that were a positive memorial in remembering the miraculous crossing of the Jordan, the stones at the Valley of Achor served as a negative memorial. Other negative memorials are recorded in 8:29 and in 2 Samuel 18:17.

It is important to notice the Lord's response to the stoning: "the LORD turned from his fierce anger" (7:26). The Lord was pleased with the fact that the nation had turned from sin by judging the sin in their midst. This episode clearly indicates that sin is serious in the sight of God and that He hates and judges sin.

2. Victory at Ai (8:1–29)

a) Promise of victory (8:1–2)

Since Israel's sin had been dealt with, the nation could once again prepare for the Lord's blessing. The Lord encouraged Joshua, saying, "Do not be afraid; do not be discouraged" (8:1). The phrase is reminiscent of 1:9 where the explanation is given why Joshua need not fear: the Lord would be with him. The Lord now commanded Joshua to attack Ai, for He had given Israel the victory. Now, however, they were to "take the whole army," in contrast to the small group that originally went up against Ai (cf. 7:3).

The Israelites were commanded to destroy Ai just as they had destroyed Jericho; however, in this campaign they were permitted to plunder the wealth of the city for themselves. Israel had previously enjoyed the spoils of war (Deut. 2:35; 3:7); now the Lord was giving them the booty of Ai. The spoils of Jericho had not been given to Israel because as the firstfruits of the land, Jericho wholly belonged to the Lord (see comments on 6:16–19). In contrast, Israel was able to receive the fruits of war at Ai. Had Achan waited, he would have enjoyed the material benefits in a correct manner!

b) Plan of attack (8:3–9)

A superficial reading may cause these verses to appear confusing concerning the number of fighting men and the description of the ambush. This has led some to suggest that the text contains a contradic-

As we read verse 2-17

tion or scribal error. A closer examination, however, discloses that Joshua describes the Israelite army divided into three groups rather than two.[22] The first group of warriors numbered 30,000. These men were sent to Ai by night, ready to ambush it from behind (8:3–4). Joshua himself would lead a decoy group of soldiers, who would draw out the warriors of Ai in order to render the city defenseless (vv. 5–6). Having gained confidence from their previous victory, the men of Ai would take the initiative in attacking Joshua's group. Joshua would feign defeat by retreating, thus drawing the men of Ai out of the city and away from it. With the men of Ai gone, the 30,000 would rise up at the appointed signal to attack the city and burn it. The third group was stationed between Ai and Bethel to prevent Bethel from assisting Ai since there was an alliance between the two (v. 12). This would enable the 30,000 to seize the city and destroy it with fire.

Joshua followed the instruction of the Lord, sending the 30,000 away by night.

c) Procedure for ambush (8:10–17)

In the morning the plan was put into action. Joshua led his contingent forward to Ai in full view of the city's inhabitants (8:10–11). In carrying out his plan, Joshua had sent 5,000 men to prevent Bethel from assisting Ai (v. 12). When the king of Ai saw the challenge, he accepted! Being confident because of their earlier victory, the men of Ai rushed out of the city against the taunting Israelites. They ran to meet Israel in battle at a place overlooking the Arabah, which denotes the Jordan Valley depression. But the king of Ai was unaware of the ambush that awaited him (v. 14).

Having lured the men of Ai out of the city, Joshua feigned defeat and fled toward the desert. The desert was the arid area that was out of the central hill country where rain fell.[23] Verses 16–17 emphasize the complete removal of any defense force from Ai. The mention of Bethel indicates that the Bethelites were being engaged in warfare by the

---

[22]Gray, for example, suggests 30,000 should read 3,000 and is to be equated with the 5,000 of 8:12. Cf. Gray, *Joshua, Judges and Ruth*, p. 90 (cf. H. G. May, "Joshua," *Peake's Commentary on the Bible*. London: Thomas Nelson and Sons Ltd., 1962, p. 295). A number of conservative writers indicate there are three distinct Israelite groups, with two different groups set in ambush. Cf. Davis, *Conquest and Crisis*, pp. 56–57; Irving L. Jensen, *Joshua: Rest-Land Won* (Chicago: Moody Press, 1966), pp. 72–73; Rea, "Joshua," p. 215; Blair, "Joshua," p. 241.

[23]For a thorough discussion of the desert (*midbar*) and related terms, see Baly, *Geography of the Bible*, pp. 101–111. Baly emphasizes two concepts in the Hebrew term: "that of *wildness* and that of the place where man is *bewildered*, confused, disoriented" (p. 103).

5,000 who had gone up to prevent their assisting Ai. The result was that Ai lay exposed to invasion by the 30,000 who waited in ambush behind the city.

d) *Pursuit of the enemy* (8:18–23)

When the men of Ai were drawn out of the city, the Lord instructed Joshua to hold out his javelin. This was the signal for the ambush party to attack Ai. Something conspicuous about Joshua's spear enabled the ambush party to see it. Perhaps the spear had a flag or banner attached to it, but a more plausible suggestion is that the sun's rays reflected from the uplifted spear, enabling the ambush party to receive the signal to attack the city.

At the sight of Joshua's uplifted javelin, the men who were hiding behind the city rose quickly and attacked. Having captured the city, they set fire to it. Just as Joshua had previously signaled the ambush party with his gleaming javelin, so now the ambush party signaled Joshua through the smoke of the burning city that their venture had been a success.

As the men of Ai turned around, they saw the smoke ascending from their city. They were in a hard place and had no power to flee. The term translated "chance" (8:20 KJV, "power"; NASB, "place") is literally "hands," which signified strength (cf. Deut. 32:36). The men of Ai had no strength to flee this way or that. If they advanced, they would face Joshua and his army; if they retreated, they would encounter the ambush party that had destroyed their city.

Joshua turned from his retreat and assaulted the enemy (8:21). Meanwhile, the ambush party advanced from the burning city to engage the enemy from the west. The Israelites slew the Aiites, "leaving them neither survivors nor fugitives" (v. 22). The thoroughness of the destruction is seen in the dual phrase. Only the king of Ai was taken alive and brought to Joshua. The king, as representative of opposition and rebellion against the Lord, would face disgrace, humiliation, and death.

e) *Plunder of the city* (8:24–29)

Having killed all of Ai's men of war in battle, the Israelites returned to the city of Ai and completed the slaughter of the remaining people. The summary statement of 8:25 records that 12,000 people fell in battle—the entire population. As Israel's commander-in-chief, Joshua's responsibility was to make sure no Aiites survived, thus he did not withdraw the signal to attack (his uplifted javelin) until all the enemy had been destroyed. The upraised hand of Joshua is reminiscent of Moses' upraised hands in the battle against the Amalekites (Exod. 17:11–12).

In contrast to the disobedience of Achan at Jericho, the Israelites obeyed the word of the Lord regarding the spoils, taking only the permissible things (cf. 8:2, 27). It appears that the deed and death of Achan had not been forgotten; his sin was not about to be repeated.

In completing the conquest, Joshua burned Ai, establishing the city as a negative memorial. The city remained a desolation at least until the writing of Joshua; it no doubt served as a vivid reminder to all passers-by of the power of the God of Israel. The second act of Joshua, which indicated the completion of Ai's conquest, was the public humiliation of the king. It was the Oriental custom to slay the king and then publicly expose his body by hanging it on a gibbet or impaling it on a stake. A modern example of this was the public humiliation of the body of Benito Mussolini at the conclusion of World War II. The public display of the dead body of the king served at least two purposes: (1) It made the conquest a vivid reality while subjecting the enemy to humiliation and defeat. (2) It struck terror into the hearts of the surrounding people.

The act was carried out according to Deuteronomy 21:22, where both the death and humiliation of the rebel is demanded. The one who is put to shame by hanging on a tree is "under God's curse" in that shameful, public act (v. 23). This public shame prefigures the work of Jesus Christ, who became a curse for all humanity by becoming the substitute Sin-Bearer for all the world (Gal. 3:13).

According to the law, it was necessary to remove the body of the king before sundown (Deut. 21:23), lest the land be defiled. As in the case of Achan (7:26), Joshua erected a heap of stones over the body of the king of Ai to negatively memorialize the rebellion against the God of Israel (8:29).

f) *Praise of God* (8:30–35)

This conclusion to the conquest of Ai was of utmost significance. The Israelites marched northward about thirty miles to Mount Ebal. The act of worship that Israel would carry out was in accord with the Lord's command in Deuteronomy 11:26–30 and 27:2–8. This was "a symbolical setting up of the law of the Lord to be the invariable rule of life to the people of Israel in the land of Canaan."[24]

[24]Keil and Delitzsch, *Joshua, Judges, Ruth*, p. 89.

The trek northward would readily have been made in two days or less. Scripture indicates (from silence) that the journey was without incident, and this no doubt was due to the fact that news of Israel's conquest of Jericho and Ai had gone before them. The inhabitants of the land would have been filled with fear. In addition, Israel's warriors would have traveled with the group, enabling Israel to defeat any opposition. An interesting point is that Israel will have occupied Shechem, which lay in the valley between Mount Ebal to the north and Mount Gerizim to the south; yet there is no mention of any battle. Perhaps the best solution is that there was a lapse of time between Israel's conquest of Ai and her sojourn to Shechem. In this interval a contingent of Israelite forces moved north, subjugating the area and enabling the worshiping Israelites to venture north in peace.[25]

As the first act of worship, Joshua built an altar to the Lord on Mount Ebal (8:30). Ebal was the higher of the two mountains, rising to a height of 3,080 feet—a suitable location for Israel's offerings. Here Israel offered burnt offerings and fellowship offerings to the Lord. This was important because in this first act of worship in the land, Israel renewed her covenant relationship to the Lord. The nation had been bound to the Lord at Sinai in a suzerainty-vassal treaty (Exod. 19:3–8) and now affirmed it.

It is interesting to note that both the burnt and fellowship offerings were voluntary offerings (Lev. 1:1–17; 3:1–17). The burnt offering signified a complete dedication to the Lord—the surrender of the entire person, in this case, the nation. The fellowship offering was one of thanksgiving, indicating peace with God had been established and the offerer was now enjoying fellowship with God.[26]

The altar was to be constructed of uncut stones (cf. Exod. 20:25). The uncut stone represented the earth as God had created it; any attempt to improve God's creation would profane it.

As a second act of worship Joshua inscribed a copy of the law on large

---

[25]Wood argues this point for three reasons: "One is that the account of the Ebal-Gerizim ceremony (Josh. 8:30) begins with the word 'then' ('az not merely the simple conjunction waw), which could imply lapse of sufficient time for such an intervening conquest. Another is that Joshua 11:19 states that no city other than Gibeon (Josh. 9) capitulated to Israel peacefully, which means that Shechem must have been taken forcibly. And a third is that Joshua 12:17, 18, 24 lists kings of the Shechem area who were killed by Joshua's troops sometime and so probably here at this logical juncture" (Wood, A Survey of Israel's History, p. 178).

[26]For the classic interpretation of the offerings, see Andrew Jukes, The Law of the Offerings (Grand Rapids: Kregel, n.d. reprint).

stones (8:32). He probably inscribed a major portion of Exodus through Deuteronomy on the stones. The mechanics of this work may be indicated by the inscription of the Code of Hammurabi that occurs on a stone seven feet high and contains 3,654 lines of text with fifty-one columns. According to Deuteronomy 27:2, the stones would have been plastered to facilitate the writing.

The inscription of the law was a further act whereby Israel affirmed their commitment to the Mosaic covenant. By writing a copy of the law, Israel indicated that they were putting themselves under the law and were affirming their intention to keep the law.

The third act of worship was the pronouncement of the cursings and blessings on the two mountains. Israel had previously been commanded to gather six tribes (Simeon, Levi, Judah, Issachar, Joseph, and Benjamin) on Mount Gerizim to bless the people (Deut. 27:12). The blessings that were conditioned on obedience are enumerated in Deuteronomy 28:1–14. The other six tribes (Reuben, Gad, Asher, Zebulun, Dan, and Naphtali) were to stand on Mount Ebal and utter the curses (Deut. 27:13). The curses—which would be the Lord's chastisement upon His people because of their disobedience—are cited in detail in Deuteronomy 27:15–26 and 28:15–68. The conditional nature of the covenant is seen in the stipulations and promises: "*If* you fully obey the LORD your God. . . . All these blessings will come upon you" (Deut. 28:1–2). "*If* you do not obey the LORD your God . . . all these curses will come upon you and overtake you" (Deut. 28:15).[27]

The indication is that the leaders of Israel (the elders, officers, and judges) stood around the ark in the middle of the valley while half the people stood on the slopes of Ebal and the other six tribes stood on the slopes of Gerizim to the south (8:33). Evidently Joshua had the Levitical priests read the law, the specifics of which are explained by the phrase "the blessing and the curses" (v. 34). Joshua in all probability did not actually read the law himself, but entrusted the reading to those who were commanded to do so (Deut. 27:14f.). "Persons are often said in Scripture to do that which they only command to be done."[28] The six tribes on Ebal responded "amen" to the cursings, while the other six tribes on Gerizim responded "amen" to the proclamation of the blessings.

---

[27]For an important distinction between the nature of conditional and unconditional covenants see J. Dwight Pentecost, *Things To Come* (Grand Rapids: Zondervan, 1958), p. 65ff.

[28]Jamieson, "Joshua," p. 23.

The extent of the reading of the law was restricted to "the blessing and the curses" (Deut. 27–28). The pronouncement was in the hearing of all the community of Israel—the assembly of Israel, the women, the little ones, and the strangers among them (8:35). The description of this audience is a further explanation of the term "all Israel" in verse 33.

The location of the proclamation of the cursings and blessings was also significant. It was given in the center of the land. This strategic location indicated that the law of God was going forth into the entire land and that the entire nation was binding itself to the stipulations of the Mosaic covenant. It was a symbolic gesture of their covenantal commitment.

For Further Study

1. Acquaint yourself with the geographical features of Joshua 6–7. Locate the following on a map: Jericho, Ai, Bethel, Shechem, Mount Ebal and Mount Gerizim.

2. Read the sections on Jericho and Ai in a geography of Bible lands to understand the physical features of the area.

3. Do the elaborate preparations, organization, and instructions have anything to say to the way things should be done in service for the Lord?

4. Cite as many lessons as you can regarding success and failure in the story of Achan.

5. Compare and contrast the victories at Jericho and Ai. Discuss the relationship between divine provision (as at Jericho) and human responsibility (as at Ai).

Chapter 7

The Southern Campaign
(Joshua 9:1–10:43)

With the conquest of Jericho and Ai, the Israelites captured a strong-hold in the central hill country of Palestine. Moreover, with this central thrust, they had succeeded in dividing the land in two. The result *into the* of Israel's penetration into the land was twofold: (1) some of their ene- *Central* mies formed an alliance, determined to impede the progress of the *hill* invaders; (2) others, namely the Gibeonites, were prepared to surren- *county* der to the invaders. *of Palestine*

The second segment of Israel's conquest traces the southern thrust of Israel into the land.

A. Deception of the Gibeonites (9:1–27)

Israel was prepared for battle but not for deception and trickery. The *our enemy the devil* Gibeonites were able to save their lives by deceiving the Israelites. *works on this lines to slow* However, the failure of the Israelites is clearly seen inasmuch as they *our* neglected to consult the Lord in the matter (9:14). *growth*

in the Life & Full Salvation

1. Introduction (9:1–2)

These two opening verses form an introduction to chapters 9–11. The inhabitants of the land formed an alliance to oppose Israel and came from three major areas: "the hill country," the ridge of mountains running north and south in the central ridge of the land; "the western foothills," the Shephelah, lying between the hill country and the coast; and the "coast" where the Canaanites dwelt. The alliance was designed to show the united thrust of the enemies against Israel.

2. *Deception of the Gibeonites* (9:3–13)

Upon hearing what Joshua had done to Jericho and Ai, the inhabitants of Gibeon devised a cunning plan to save their lives. They had to act quickly, for they could expect an Israelite invasion momentarily because of their close proximity to the invaders. The city of Gibeon lay six and a half miles southwest of Ai and six miles northwest of Jerusalem. Gibeon has been identified as el-Jib and has been confirmed by the findings of archaeologist J. B. Pritchard. He discovered numerous jar handles on the site with the inscription "Gibeon." The jars were used in the city's wine industry and coincide with the rich, fertile fields surrounding the hill on which Gibeon was built.

The city of Gibeon was actually a tetrapolis, consisting of the cities of Gibeon, Kephirah, Beeroth, and Kiriath Jearim (9:17). Although the four cities had combined their resources, they were nonetheless very small compared to an invading host of more than two million people. Garstang provides information suggesting their size and population.[1] Gibeon covered an area of ten acres while supporting a population of twenty-five hundred. The city of Beeroth, identified as Tell el Nasbeh, was one of the best fortified in the country. Its walls were seventeen feet thick and are still preserved to a height of twenty-eight feet. It covered eight acres, with a population of two thousand, including five hundred warriors.

Kephirah was also a well-fortified, readily defended city on a plateau jutting out toward the coastal plain. It occupied five acres which indicates a population of perhaps 1,250 people. Kiriath Jearim covered six acres and had about fifteen hundred inhabitants.

The city of Gibeon was the center of the alliance, indicating the city's importance. It was later to become important in Israel's history as a Levitical city (Josh. 21:17), and later as the site of the tabernacle (1 Kings 3:4; 1 Chron. 16:39).

The Gibeonites and Hivites are referred to synonymously (cf. 9:3, 7). It is also generally assumed that the Hivites are synonymous with the Horites, equivalent to the extra-biblical Hurrians. Some reject the latter association, however.

When the Gibeonites heard what Joshua and the Israelites "had done to Jericho and Ai, they resorted to a ruse" (9:3–4). As Joshua had acted craftily in a military sense, so the Gibeonites acted craftily in a

---

[1] Garstang, *Joshua-Judges*, pp. 162–167.

different sense. They posed as ambassadors from a distant country. Their "worn-out" items were to suggest a long journey. The terms "worn" and "old" indicate their strategy: "worn-out sacks," "old wineskins," "worn and patched sandals," and "old clothes" (vv. 4–5). The wineskins were, literally, "tied up" (9:4), which suggests the method of repairing broken wineskins. When a rupture occurred in a bag (a goat's skin), the torn piece was tied up in the form of a bag so that the major part of the bag could continue to be used. This method of repair (rather than inserting a patch) was adopted to indicate that the bags were torn during a long journey. Even the bread of the Gibeonites was dry and moldy.[2]

The Gibeonites came to the Israelite camp at Gilgal and lied, saying they had come from a distant country. They asked Joshua for a covenant of peace (9:6). The term "covenant" (berith) indicates

> a legally binding obligation . . . the particular nature of which is to be determined . . . on the parties concerned. . . . (Generally) one party takes the initiative and comes to terms with the other. But the net result is still a 'partnership,' an agreement voluntarily accepted by both parties.[3]

The covenant obligated Israel in her relationship with the Gibeonites.

The Israelites' initial response indicated their hesitancy. They recognized the possibility of deception (9:7). But the Gibeonites assuaged the fear of the Israelites by responding, "We are your servants" (v. 8). This was simply "a phrase intended to secure the favour of Joshua, and by no means implied a readiness on their part to submit to the Israelites and pay them tribute."[4]

Joshua appeared dissatisfied with the Gibeonites' response and demanded to know who they were and where they had come from (9:8). In their response, the Gibeonites indicated they had come from a distant country out of respect for the name of the Lord, Israel's God. Surely Joshua would not harm those who had come out of reverence for the name of the Lord! In their statement about having heard of the

---

[2] Robert Jamieson provides insight: "This must have been that commonly used by travellers—a sort of biscuit made in the form of large rings, about an inch thick and four or five inches in diameter. Not being so well baked as our biscuits, it becomes hard and mouldy, from the moisture left in the dough. It is usually soaked in water previous to being used." Robert Jamieson, "Joshua," *A Commentary Critical, Experimental, and Practical on the Old and New Testaments* (Grand Rapids: Eerdmans, 1945 reprint), p. 24.
[3] J. Barton Payne, *The Theology of the Older Testament* (Grand Rapids: Zondervan Publishing House, 1962), pp. 79–80.
[4] Keil and Delitzsch, *Joshua, Judges, Ruth,* p. 97.

Lord's acts on behalf of Israel, the Gibeonites wisely omitted anything that pertained to the Jordan crossing and the recent conquest. These events were too recent to have spread abroad. Had they mentioned them, they would have exposed themselves as being from the immediate vicinity. In concluding their appeal, the Gibeonites reminded the Israelites of their crumbled bread and torn wineskins as proof that they had come from a distant country (vv. 12–13).

3. Declaration with the Gibeonites (9:14–15)

Israel's response is seen in 9:14, which appears also as a key statement in explaining Israel's failure: they neglected to consult the Lord. Failure to consult the Lord in a decision resulted in disaster, for they concluded an agreement with the enemy. How would the Lord have made the matter known? He probably would have spoken through the Urim and Thummim (cf. Num. 27:21). As a result, Joshua concluded a peace agreement with the Gibeonites (9:15). It is possible to see a relationship between verses 14 and 15, that is, the making of the covenant in verse 15 is explained through the phrase, "Israel sampled their provisions" (9:14). Enacting a covenant through eating together has a precedent in other passages. Jacob and Abimelech inaugurated a covenant by eating together (Gen. 26:26–31); Jacob and Laban were reconciled and also enacted a covenant through eating together (Gen. 31:44, 54).[5]

Joshua's peace agreement with the Gibeonites assured them of their physical safety. The phrase "to let them live" was the major point of the covenant and explains "made a treaty of peace" (9:15). The fact that Israel was allowing the Gibeonites to remain alive is cited because Israel ought to have exterminated them in obedience to the command of God.

Although Joshua had been tricked and did not realize they were Gibeonites, he nonetheless sinned by not consulting the Lord. The sin led to wrong actions—making the covenant. The Lord had given distinct stipulations concerning Israel's relationship with other nations: (1) they were permitted to enact a peace treaty with those of a far country, although those people would be forced to serve Israel as slaves (Deut. 20:11, 15); (2) Israel was not allowed to enter into peace treaties with those living nearby (Exod. 23:32–33); instead, they were to destroy them (Deut. 7:2, 16).

---

[5]An alternate suggestion is that the Israelites simply tested the bread to see if it was as old as the Gibeonites claimed.

4. Discovery of Israel (9:16–21)

At the conclusion of the covenant, the Gibeonites must have returned to their home cities. Three days later, the Israelites discovered they had been tricked. They immediately set out to deal with the deceivers. When Israel arrived at the cities of the Gibeonites, they realized the reality of the deception but kept their word by permitting the Gibeonites to remain alive. The reason for Israel's faithfulness to the covenant with the Gibeonites was that they "had sworn an oath to them by the LORD, the God of Israel" (9:18–19). Israel had made the oath in the name of the Lord, and if they had broken the covenant, they would have dishonored the name of the Lord and brought His name into disrepute. To preserve the integrity of the Lord's name, Israel had to keep her word. We know that Israel did right in keeping this covenant, for later in Israel's history Saul broke this covenant, and put some Gibeonites to death. As a consequence of Saul's action, God judged the nation with a famine (2 Sam. 21:1–2).

Israel no longer had an alternative regarding the lives of the Gibeonites. Israel did, however, have the opportunity to prevent the Gibeonites from leading them into idolatry and they accomplished this by forcing the Gibeonites to perform menial service. Thus Israel reduced the Gibeonites to slavery, forcing them to be hewers of wood and drawers of water (9:21; cf. Deut. 29:10–11).

5. Decree of Joshua (9:22–27)

Realizing he had been tricked, Joshua summoned the Gibeonites, reminding them of what they had done. The Israelite leader then pronounced a curse on them: they were set apart to perpetual servitude as hewers of wood and drawers of water for the tabernacle, a menial service for the aliens in the midst of Israel (Deut. 29:11).

There were several implications to the punishment: (1) The Gibeonites would be Israel's servants in manual labor perpetually (cf. 1 Chron. 9:2; Ezra 2:43, 58). (2) They would be servants of Israel's God, as indicated by Joshua's emphasis that they would be slaves "for the house of *my* God" (9:23). Their service in the tabernacle would be a continual reminder to them of the true God, whom they would acknowledge by their actions. Their forced acknowledgment of the Lord would prefigure a great day in the future when all mankind will acknowledge the Lord (Phil. 2:10). (3) As Israel's servants, the Gibeonites would not be in a position to entice Israel to sin. In this curse the prophecy of Noah would be literally fulfilled (Gen. 9:25).

Following the pronouncement of punishment, the Gibeonites acknowledged their deceitfulness and explained that they had misled Israel to preserve their lives (9:24). They had heard of God's command to Moses that Israel was to exterminate all the inhabitants of the land (Deut. 20:16–17). Now, having concluded a covenant of peace, they readily submitted to the Israelites. Joshua kept the enacted agreement and assigned them to the manual service in the tabernacle. They did not begin their service immediately, but did so as soon as the Lord designated a location for the tabernacle.

B. Defeat of the Amorites (10:1–43)

1. Cause of the conflict (10:1–5)

The capitulation of the Gibeonites was significant, for Gibeon lay just northwest of Jerusalem, making Jerusalem vulnerable to attack. Gibeon thus provided a stronghold in the central hill country of the land. This threat precipitated an alliance among the Amorites in which Adoni-Zedek, king of Jerusalem, united with the other Amorite kings against Israel. Adoni-Zedek literally means "my Lord is righteous," and appears to have been the name of an Amorite deity, as well as the title of the king of Jerusalem.

> Adoni-zedek was probably a rather powerful king and an influential one in central Palestine. The Amarna Letters indicate that Jerusalem was the center of political activity in the fourteenth century B.C. and was always conscious of its own security.[6]

The Amorites were a nomadic people, one major group dwelling in the area that later was to be Judah, while another group dwelt on the east side of the Jordan, from considerably south of the Dead Sea to north of the Sea of Galilee. In a Sumerian hymn to the god of the west, the following is said of the Amorites:

> The weapon is (his) companion . . .
> Who knows no submission,
> Who eats uncooked flesh,
> Who has no house in his life-time,
> Who does not bury his dead companion[7]

---

[6]Davis, *Conquest and Crisis*, p. 63.

[7]William Foxwell Albright, *From the Stone Age to Christianity* (Garden City, N.Y.: Doubleday Anchor Books, 1957), p. 166.

The Amorite nomads were wild and savage compared to the Egyptians and Accadians. The men were armed with composite bows, heavy throw-sticks, and javelins. For most of the year the Amorites depended on pasturage for their herds of cattle, sheep, goats, and donkeys; in addition, they depended on hunting and raids for food. Throughout most of the year they lived in the Palestinian hill country or wherever they could obtain food for their herds.[8]

The Amorites were portrayed as awesome foes: "Though he was tall as the cedars and strong as the oaks" (Amos 2:9). But they represented more than a physical menace to Israel.

> The Baals and Ashtartes and other 'gods' whose worship seemed always to threaten to infiltrate the true worship of Yahweh are the 'gods of the Amorites' (Josh. 24:15; Judg. 6:10).[9]

When Adoni-Zedek heard of the alliance between Israel and Gibeon, he was alarmed because he saw the pact as a potential threat to the security of his own city of Jerusalem. He knew that Gibeon was a great city, larger than Ai. Although Jerusalem was a major stronghold, having valleys to the south, east and west, it was vulnerable from the north, where Gibeon was located. Therefore Adoni-Zedek formed an alliance with the kings of Hebron, Jarmuth, Lachish, and Eglon in an attempt to stop the progress of Israel.

The attack launched against Gibeon by the Amorite alliance had a twofold purpose: (1) The alliance intended to punish Gibeon for submitting to Israel (10:4). (2) They intended to stop Israel's advance to the south.

2. *Course of the conflict* (10:6–15)

a) *Miracle of the hailstones* (10:6–11)

The Gibeonites were at a decided advantage. Having made a covenant with Israel, they were under the protection of that nation. Thus when the Amorite league threatened Gibeon, the latter appealed to the Israelites for help. The urgency of the situation is seen in Gibeon's request, "Do not abandon your servants" (10:6; literally, "slacken not your hands from your servants"). The need was immediate, for the Amorite invaders stood on the threshold of Gibeon.

Before the Israelites tried to overcome the Amorite league, they received direction from the Lord (10:8). This was important, for they

---

[8]Ibid.
[9]Hoffner, "Amorites," ZPEB, vol. 1, p. 143.

could have gone up and suffered defeat if they had ignored the counsel of the Lord. The Lord's directive was similar to the counsel He gave prior to the second invasion of Ai (cf. 8:1). He exhorted the Israelites not to fear because He was giving the enemy into their hands.

Since Israel was still encamped at Gilgal, they were twenty-five miles from Gibeon. Their strategy included marching all night from Gilgal and coming upon the Amorites "by surprise" in the morning (10:9). Joshua routed the confused enemy and pursued them westward to Beth Horon, which lay five miles to the west of Gibeon. The Amorites then fled southwestward on the road to Azekah, which was fifteen miles southwest of Beth Horon. During the hot pursuit the Israelite soldiers cut down the fleeing Amorites with their swords. Azekah lay in the foothills between the central mountain ridge and the coastal plain. From there the remaining Amorites fled to Makkedah, which was located in the plains.

When the Amorites were fleeing from Beth Horon to Azekah, the Lord rained hailstones on them, and more died from hailstones than from Israelite swords (10:11). This was a further confirmation that the Lord was with Joshua just as He had been with Moses (Josh. 1:5). In the seventh plague in Egypt, the Lord had vindicated His servant Moses and His people Israel by sending hail on the Egyptians (cf. Exod. 9:24); during Israel's pursuit of the routed Amorite alliance, the Lord vindicated Joshua and His people Israel by sending hailstones on the enemy.

Several factors indicate the miraculous nature of the victory: (1) God gave supernatural strength to Israel, enabling them to fight after having marched twenty-five miles during the night. (2) The Lord rained hailstones on the Amorites (10:11). (3) More Amorites were killed by the hailstones than by Israel's swords. (4) The hailstones struck only the Amorites despite the close pursuit by the Israelites (cf. Exod. 9:25–26).

b) *Miracle of the extended day* (10:12–15)

During the battle against the Amorites God not only performed the miracle of the hailstones but also performed a spectacular miracle in Israel's behalf involving the sun. There has been considerable debate among expositors as they have struggled to interpret the command of Joshua for the sun to stand still. In his prayer in 10:12 Joshua revealed his dependence on the divine promise of verse 8 that the enemy would be delivered into his hand. Joshua prayed, "O sun, stand still over

Gibeon, O moon, over the Valley of Aijalon" (v. 12). It was probably early in the day, while the sun was rising in the east and the moon setting in the west, that Joshua prayed this unusual prayer.

God responded to the prayer of Joshua, causing the sun to stand still and the moon to stop until Israel had defeated her enemies (10:13). Scholars have offered several views in expounding this passage.

(1) The poetic view. Keil and Delitzsch, although apparently not holding this view, discuss it and suggest the possibility of poetic language:

> The poetical form of the passage in ver. 13 also leaves no doubt whatever that vers. 13 and 14 contain the words of the old poet, and are not a prose comment made by the historian upon the poetical passage quoted. The only purely historical statement is ver. 15.[10]

(2) The total eclipse view. This has been espoused by Robert Dick Wilson.[11] John Rea also mentions this view and suggests the reason for the prayer was relief from the sun.[12]

The darkening of the sun and moon was significant, for the prominent deities of the Amorites, the sun and moon, were rendered ineffective through the prayer of the Israelite leader. In this sense, the miracle is readily seen as a judgment on the heathen gods in a sense similar to the judgment on Egypt's gods (cf. Exod. 10:21–22). The judgment on the heathen nations through the engulfing darkness prefigures the tribulation period when darkness will be a form of the Lord's judgment (Isa. 13:10; Joel 2:31).

(3) The view that the light was actually prolonged for about a day. This is widely held, mostly by conservatives. Advocates believe (for the most part) that God actually extended the light for about a whole day. However, there is a disagreement concerning the manner in which the light was prolonged. One suggestion is the slowing or actual stoppage of the earth's rotation. Keil and Delitzsch mention the possibility of "a miraculous suspension of the revolution of the earth upon its axis, which would make it appear to the eye of an observer as if the sun itself were standing still"[13] A second suggestion concerning the prolongation

---

[10]Keil and Delitzsch, *Joshua, Judges, Ruth*, pp. 107–108; cf. pp. 110–111.

[11]Wilson stated, "Now, it is well known that atalu is the ordinary word in the astronomical tablets for 'eclipse' and that the verb adaru means 'to be dark.' Recalling that the radicals dm are the root of the verbs occurring in Joshua x. 12, 13, I immediately turned up the passage and at once recognized that it would make good sense to render the form dōm in Joshua's prayer by 'become dark,' or 'be eclipsed'" (Robert Dick Wilson, "What Does 'The Sun Stood Still' Mean?" *Princeton Theological Review*, XVI (1918), p. 46.

[12]Rea, "Joshua," p. 218.

[13]Keil and Delitzsch, *Joshua, Judges, Ruth*, p. 112.

of light is catastrophism. Proponents suggest there is a natural explanation for the phenomenon. Some suggest that a comet flew close to the earth (Velikovsky); others suggest the orbit of Mars was close to the earth (Patten, Hatch, and Steinhauer). In each case, the foreign body supposedly had the effect of slowing the earth's rotation. Another suggestion is the extension or refraction of the sun's rays on a local level. Davis posits this view in which he understands this event as a localized miracle. This suggestion has precedence in Scripture (2 Kings 20:10–11) where a local miracle was performed in Hezekiah's day.[14]

The language of the text demands a miracle (10:13–14). The suggestion of an eclipse appears inadequate because of the phrase, "the sun . . . delayed going down about a whole day" (v. 13). Moreover, verse 14 indicates it was a unique day, that is, the only one of its kind. An eclipse would be disqualified by the statement that there was no day like it before or since.

Joshua's concern was that the day would draw to a conclusion without Israel's having achieved a victory over the Amorites. In order to enable Israel to complete that conquest, Joshua prayed to the Lord for the day to be lengthened. As a result, the sun delayed setting for about a day.

The account of the brilliant victory was recorded in the Book of Jashar (10:13). The designation is synonymous with the Book of Wars of the Lord (Num. 21:14), describing odes of praise concerning heroes of the theocracy, together with historical notations of their achievements.[15]

At the conclusion of the victory, Joshua and the Israelites returned to their camp at Gilgal (10:15; cf. v. 43). The statement indicates Israel still maintained Gilgal as their base of operations, even though a number of other important cities had been conquered.

3. Culmination of the conflict (10:16–43)

The result of the conflict is stated in the ensuing verses.

a) Discovery of the kings (10:16–21)

Through the intervention of the Lord, the Amorite alliance was destroyed by hailstones and the swords of the Israelites. The five kings

---

[14]Davis provides a lucid discussion of these views in Conquest and Crisis, pp. 66–70. For a discussion of the catastrophic views, see Immanuel Velikovsky, Worlds in Collision (Garden City: Doubleday, 1950), and Donald W. Patten et al., The Long Day of Joshua and Six Other Catastrophes (Seattle: Pacific Meridian Publishing Company, 1973).

[15]Keil and Delitzsch, Joshua, Judges, Ruth, pp. 107–108.

fled the scene of the battle and hid in the cave at Makkedah. Caves were a common source of refuge. David fled to the cave of Adullam for refuge in his estrangement from Saul (1 Sam. 22:1f.); on another occasion, three of David's chief men came to him at the cave (2 Sam. 23:13).

When Joshua discovered the kings were hiding in the cave, he had his men roll large stones against the entrance of the cave to prevent their escape. In addition, some of his men guarded the cave. During that time the other Israelite warriors attacked the rearguard of the fleeing Amorites to prevent them from reentering their fortified cities for protection. Such was the Lord's way of delivering the Amorites into Israel's hand.

The Israelites killed most of the enemy on the battlefield although a few managed to escape and take refuge in the cities. This was short-lived, however, as the ensuing conquest completed the extermination (cf. 10:28–43). The concluding statement in verse 21 is a proverbial expression: "no one uttered (literally, "sharpened his tongue") a word against the Israelites" (cf. Exod. 11:7). The meaning is that no one dared harm any of the Israelites.

b) *Destruction of the kings* (10:22–27)

When the Israelite army commanders returned from their conquest, Joshua gave the order to bring forth the five kings of the Amorites from the cave. Calling the Israelite military leaders, Joshua had them place their feet on the necks of the conquered kings (10:24). To the western mind this appears unusual, but to the easterner this was a common military custom. Both Assyrian and Egyptian sculpture portray their kings dominating their enemies by placing their feet on the necks of their enemies. This is also the picture of Messiah at His Second Advent (Ps. 110:1).

This unusual act had several important points of significance: (1) It was a sign of Israel's complete subjection of the enemy and symbolized the success of the conquest. (2) It was designed to motivate the Israelites to gain further victories over the Canaanites (10:25).

Joshua followed this act with a word of encouragement to the military leaders that was reminiscent of God's encouragement to Joshua (10:25; cf. 1:7, 9).

As a finale to the battle with the Amorites, Joshua slew the five kings and hung them on five trees until evening. This was a further ignominious act designed to add shame and humiliation to the already defeated Amorites. At evening, the bodies were taken down in accord with the Mosaic Law (Deut. 21:22–23). The corpses were then thrown into the cave where the kings had hidden and left unburied. To leave a corpse unburied was the highest possible insult that could be perpetrated—even on an enemy.[16]

c) *Destruction of the cities* (10:28–39)

1) *Makkedah* (10:28)

At this point Joshua conducted a swift raid into the south country in order to destroy the strength of the inhabitants without necessarily occupying their cities. During the campaign Joshua leveled his attacks against the key cities. At the conclusion he led his army back to the base at Gilgal (10:43). Later some of the cities had to be recaptured.

The people of Makkedah were all put to death (10:28), and the king suffered the same fate as the king of Jericho—he was impaled (cf. 8:2, 29).

2) *Libnah* (10:29–30)

"All Israel" here does not refer to all 2½ million people but to all the men of war. Libnah has been identified as Tell es-Safi, approximately seven miles almost due north of Lachish. Libnah is the point where the valley known as the Vale of Elah ("Terebinth Valley") connects the Judean highlands with the Philistine plain.[17] The name given it by the Crusaders—"Blanchegarde"—indicates the peculiarity of the region. Its white limestone cliffs face west twelve miles across the plain to Ashdod. This made it a formidable location.[18]

The same destructive work was done to Libnah as to Jericho and Makkedah.

3) *Lachish* (10:31–33)

Lachish was probably the strongest city of the confederacy of Lachish, Eglon, and Hebron. It has been identified at Tell ed-Duweir, a

---

[16]Kelley comments, "According to ancient Semitic belief, the dead who received no proper burial, or whose grave was disturbed, found no resting-place in Sheol. Every disaster befell the man who was not buried in the grave of his fathers. When the prophet Jeremiah wished to pronounce a curse on Jehoiakim, he did so by declaring that 'with the burial of an ass he shall be buried, dragged and cast forth beyond the gates of Jerusalem' (Jer. 22:19), and that 'his dead body shall be cast out to the heat by day and the frost by night' (Jer. 36:30).

Many ancient graves bore inscriptions invoking a curse on those who dared disturb the dead who rested within. One Eshmunazar of Sidon, for example, prayed that he who desecrated his tomb 'might have no root beneath, or fruit above, or any beauty among the living under the sun.'" Page H. Kelley, *The Book of Amos* (Grand Rapids: Baker, 1966), pp. 37–38. Also see Roland de Vaux, *Ancient Israel* (New York: McGraw-Hill, 1965), pp. 56–61.

[17]Charles F. Pfeiffer and Howard F. Vos, *The Wycliffe Historical Geography of Bible Lands* (Chicago: Moody Press, 1967), p. 112.

[18]Smith, *Historical Geography*, pp. 160–161.

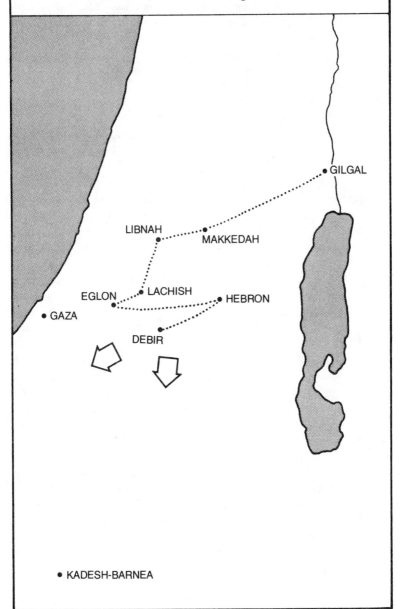

THE CONQUEST

GILGAL

LIBNAH

MAKKEDAH

EGLON LACHISH

HEBRON

GAZA

DEBIR

KADESH-BARNEA

mound of eighteen acres located fifteen miles west of Hebron.

Considerable information is available concerning the fosse temple that functioned there *c*. 1600 B.C.–1200 B.C. Gifts of ornaments, beads in ivory, glass, and alabaster lay on the offering table. Bones of birds, animals, and fish were discovered on the floor debris. The bones of the sacrificial offerings corresponded to the Israelite sacrifices (Lev. 7:32). A bronze statuette of a male deity was discovered outside. In their worship, young animals were sacrificed, gifts were placed on a cult table, fire was burned in a hearth, and libation offerings were poured out.[19]

Lachish was also defeated and totally destroyed. When the king of Gezer came with his army to help, Joshua annihilated them too. Nothing is said about the capture of Gezer.

4) *Eglon* (10:34–35)

From Lachish the Israelites moved southwestward to Eglon, an Amorite town in the western Shephelah that has been identified by William F. Albright as Tell el-Hesi. Its location was strategic, for it was near the border of the Philistine plain on the high road from Gaza to Jerusalem and controlled the valley leading down from the Shephelah.[20] Eglon was a city of considerable importance during the Bronze Age but diminished in importance after its destruction in the thirteenth century B.C.[21]

Like the other cities before it, Eglon was captured and all its inhabitants slain.

5) *Hebron* (10:36–37)

From Eglon, Israel moved due east toward Hebron, one of the oldest existing towns. When Abram came into the land, he worshiped at Hebron (Gen. 13:18). In earlier days the Hebrews called Hebron by the name of Kiriath Arba, which means "tetrapolis"; however, the identification of the other three cities is uncertain. Hebron occupied a strategic location, being situated at the most southerly road center of the highland system where the routes from Moab, the southern Negev, Egypt, and the coast met those of the interior and the north.[22] Unfortunately, little archaeological data has surfaced concerning the history of Hebron. Even the walls related to its being a city of refuge have not been discovered.

---

[19]J. Arthur Thompson, "Lachish," ZPEB, vol. 3, p. 857.
[20]Garstang, *Joshua–Judges*, p. 373.
[21]Baly, *Geography of the Bible*, p. 139.
[22]Garstang, *Joshua–Judges*, p. 373.

Joshua destroyed Hebron completely, annihilating all the inhabitants.[23]

6) *Debir* (10:38–39)

The attack on the city of Debir took the Israelites west-southwest of Hebron. In conquering Debir, Joshua left no survivors, dealing with the city as with the others.

Following an archaeological investigation by W. F. Albright and M. G. Kyle in 1926, Debir was identified with Tell Beit Mirsim, thirteen miles southwest of Hebron and seven miles south of Lachish. At this site a household stela portraying a Canaanite serpent goddess was found. She appears as a woman clad in a long robe with a large snake coiling around her.[24] This above site, however, has been disputed and recent archaeological discoveries tend to favor modern Hirbet Rabud.

d) *Destruction of the south country* (10:40–43)

Joshua's conquest is summarized in 10:40. The phrase "the whole region" is amplified in the succeeding phrases. The "hill country" is the central mountain ridge of Judea; the "Negev" is the desert region to the south; the "western foothills" refers to the Shephelah, located between the Judean hills and the coastal plain; the "mountain slopes" refers to the area sloping eastward toward the Dead Sea.

The summary statement is also important in pointing out that the conquest took place (1) at the command of the Lord, and (2) through His power (cf. 10:40, 42).

Following the destruction of the central and southern areas, Joshua moved further south in order to take complete control of the land. He fought the enemy as far south as Kadesh Barnea, which was fifty miles south of Beersheba. Gaza represented the southernmost town along the Mediterranean coastline. Goshen probably refers to a town in the southern hill country (cf. 15:51).

The southern conquest of Joshua was complete and thorough. Unfortunately, however, these initial conquests of Israel were not lasting, and later the Israelites once more battled for sites they had previously won.

---

[23]The battle for the occupation of Hebron was not concluded with Joshua. Hebron remains a city of conflict with the struggle between Jews and Arabs. Cf. *Time*, March 31, 1980, p. 38.

[24]Jack Finegan, *Light from the Ancient Past*, (Princeton: Princeton University Press, 1959), p. 140.

For Further Study

1. Read an article on the Gibeonites in a Bible dictionary or encyclopedia.

2. What lessons does the deception of the Gibeonites suggest concerning the cunning schemes of Satan (cf. Eph. 6:11)? How can you as a Christian stand fast against the deceitfulness and devices of Satan?

3. What lessons about dealing with past mistakes are suggested by the story of the Gibeonites?

4. What lessons concerning the faithfulness of God can we learn from Joshua's conquest of the land (cf. 1:6-9; 10:40-43). Cite some ways in which God has demonstrated His faithfulness to you.

5. Discuss the relationship between the sovereignty of God and the responsibility of man in the conquest of the land (note that in 10:40-41, Joshua conquered; in 10:42, the Lord conquered).

Megiddo, it occupied the most strategic position in the land, the real key to Palestine. Its situation and character accorded fully with its importance.[2]

This strategic location made Hazor the political and military hub of Palestine during this period.[3]

Ancient Hazor has been identified through excavations as Tell el-Qedah in the plain of Huleh, five miles southwest of Lake Huleh and nine or ten miles north of the Sea of Kinnereth. The site was identified by John Garstang in 1926. Hazor was a uniquely fortified enclosure. It consisted of the city proper on a mound of 25 acres rising 165 feet above the road running past it. The camp area, a level plateau, occupied a total of 170 acres—very large for that day. It was protected on two sides and partially on a third by steep watercourses. In addition, the city was surrounded on three sides by great ramparts of earth.[4]

The city had a probable population of forty thousand, with a similar number of horses and chariots. It was likely the largest city built in Palestine during the biblical period.[5] The city is mentioned in Egyptian execration texts written c. 1900 B.C.; several letters from Mari on the middle Euphrates c. 1700 B.C. mention Hazor; later it is recorded that ambassadors journeyed from Babylon to see the king of Hazor.[6] Thus Joshua's culminating battle in the northern conquest may also have been one of his most crucial battles.

Jabin's alliance involved the kings surrounding the Sea of Kinnereth (Galilee). Madon lay immediately west of the Sea of Kinnereth; Shimron was situated east of Mount Carmel, while Acshaph lay northeast of Carmel (11:1). The kings of the north "in the mountains" (v. 2) lived in the hill country of Naphtali, while the "Arabah south of Kinnereth" refers to the Jordan Rift Valley south of the Sea of Kinnereth. The "western foothills" refers to the Plain of Sharon, while "Naphoth Dor" (literally, "the heights of Dor") has reference to the foothills of Mount Carmel. Such was the area represented by the alliance of the north against Israel.

The great army that Joshua faced was "as numerous as the sand on the seashore" (11:4). According to Josephus, first-century A.D. Jewish

[2]Garstang, *Joshua-Judges,* p. 183.
[3]Coker, "Hazor," ZPEB, vol. 3, p. 50.
[4]Garstang, *Joshua-Judges,* p. 381.
[5]Coker, "Hazor," p. 50.
[6]Pfeiffer and Vos, *Wycliffe Historical Geography,* p. 131.

writer, the combined forces were 300,000 infantry, 10,000 cavalry, and 20,000 war chariots.

> The war-chariots were probably, like those of Egypt and Assyria (Neh. xi.13), made of wood . . . but nailed and tipped with iron, and armed with iron scythes affixed to the poles."[7]

In preparation for battle, the chariots were disassembled, carried over the hills to the battle site, and then reassembled and employed in battle.

The northern coalition met Israel for battle by the Waters of Merom (11:7).

> Very likely it was on the small plain by the copious spring between the modern towns of Meiron and Safed, about six miles southwest of Hazor; a wadi from the spring flows nine miles southward into the Sea of Galilee.[8]

B. Conquest of the Northern Kings (11:6–9)

Once more, as Joshua faced perhaps the greatest battle of his life, the Lord encouraged him, promising Israel victory in their battle (11:6). Moreover, the Lord gave instructions to Israel to hamstring the enemy's horses—to cut their leg tendons so as to cripple them and make then ineffective in warfare; yet the animals would still be useful for domestic purposes. In addition, Israel was to burn the enemy's chariots. Why was this command given? Wouldn't the chariots have been useful for Israel in future warfare? It was to remind Israel that the Lord gave them their success, not their military prowess. Should they have kept war-horses and chariots, they would have depended on their own military strength rather than trusting the Lord for victory. This ultimately happened to Solomon (1 Kings 10:28; cf. Deut. 17:16).

A key word in 11:7 concerning the methodology of the victory is "suddenly," which indicates the encounter involved the element of surprise. Garstang has reconstructed the scene.[9] Jabin's chariots had been disassembled for transportation to Merom. Joshua conducted a forced march that brought the Israelites into confrontation with the northern kings sooner than they had anticipated. In the surprise attack, the chariots proved worthless because they were disassembled. Meanwhile, the Israelite invaders assigned men to run up and down the

---

[7]Jamieson, "Joshua," p. 31.
[8]Rea, "Joshua," p. 220.
[9]Garstang, *Joshua-Judges*, pp. 196–198.

tethering lines, maiming and perhaps liberating the horses. The horses, no doubt, stampeded, causing a panic. Amid the confusion, the northern kings were an easy prey for Israel.

The reason for the complete victory for Israel was that the Lord delivered the enemy into their hands (11:8). The extent of the victory was such that Israel pursued the fleeing enemy as far as Greater Sidon, which lies on the Mediterranean Sea, considerably north of Hazor; Misrephoth Maim, due west of Hazor, on the Mediterranean Sea; and to the Valley of Mizpeh to the east. No enemy soldier survived.

The victory of Israel was complete—as was Israel's obedience in hamstringing the horses and burning the chariots. It was a sign that Joshua and his people were willing to trust the Lord.

C. Capture of Hazor (11:10–15)

The capture of Hazor was perhaps the most important conquest of all, for it was the largest, strongest city in the land. Only the Lord's miraculous deliverance could have given the Israelites control of Hazor (cf. 11:8). Israel was not familiar with siege warfare; yet the conquest of Hazor would have demanded this with her huge earth ramparts.

As was true of other captured peoples, all the inhabitants of Hazor were devoted to destruction. Joshua concluded the battle by burning the city—something he had not done to any other city of the northern campaign (11:13). Joshua refrained from burning the other cities (apart from Jericho and Ai in the central campaign) so that they could be later occupied. Perhaps he burned Hazor to teach a psychological lesson: "People would be forced to recognize that any city could have been burned had Israel so chosen, if great Hazor could not escape."[10]

The northern area was probably taken more quickly than the south.

> The fact that Jabin made an alliance to withstand Israel aided Joshua in this full conquest, even as the alliance of the south had helped there. If Joshua had not been able to defeat the strength of the North in one major blow, the individual subjugation of each city would have occupied a much longer time. As it was, the northern campaign appears to have taken even less time than the southern.[11]

As in the capture of Ai, Israel had the privilege of taking the spoils from Hazor (cf. 8:2, 27). The fact that Israel was obedient in all these matters is seen in the summary statement of 11:15. Obedience was the underlying factor for the nation's success.

---

[10]Wood, *Survey of Israel's History*, p. 184.
[11]Ibid., pp. 184–185.

For Further Study

1. Locate Hazor on a map and read an article on Hazor in a Bible dictionary or encyclopedia.

2. Discuss the significance of Joshua's greatest test at Hazor. What benefits can testings have for the believer (cf. James 1:2–3)?

3. Why did the Lord encourage Joshua at precisely the moment before the major battle (11:6)? Study Paul's experience in prison concerning the Lord's timing in encouragement (2 Tim. 4:17).

4. What place does obedience have in the Christian's life (cf. Matt. 7:24; James 1:22–25).

Chapter 9

Summary of the Conquest
(Joshua 11:16–12:24)

A. Summary of the Conquered Territory (11:16–23)

The statement in 11:16 indicates Joshua conquered the entire territory. The comment is similar to the statement of 10:40–41. Joshua conquered southern Canaan: the hill country of Judah, the Negev region to the south, the region of Goshen (probably between Gaza and Gibeon; see comment on 10:41), the western foothills (between the coastal plain and Judean hills), and the Arabah, which likely refers to the Jordan Rift Valley south of the Dead Sea to the Gulf of Aqaba. The area called the mountains of Israel is distinct from the hill country mentioned earlier in 11:16 and refers to a region in the north.

The extremities of Joshua's conquest are stated in 11:16. Mount Halak, lying twenty-five miles south of Beersheba, represents the southern boundary. The name Halak means "bald" or "bare" and has been identified as the modern Jebel Halaq. It was situated toward Seir, the Edomite territory west of the Arabah. The northern extremity of the conquest was Baal Gad at the foot of Mount Hermon, the majestic mountain that rises to more than nine thousand feet above sea level and lies north of the Sea of Kinnereth and north of Dan.

In all this territory—from Halak to Hermon—Joshua was merciless in destroying all the kings and native people.

Joshua's conquest took "a long time"—about seven years (11:18; see comments on 14:10). The reason the conquest took as long as it did was that only Gibeon submitted peacefully; all the other cities had to be taken through warfare (v. 19).

99

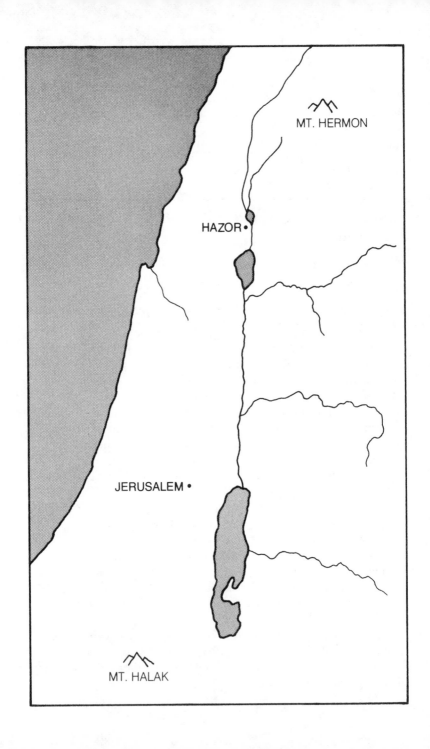

The other cities did not surrender to Israel due to the reason given in 11:20: "For it was the LORD himself who hardened their hearts to wage war against Israel, so that he might destroy them totally." Augustine comments, "Because the Israelites had shown mercy to some of them of their own accord, though in opposition to the command of God, therefore it is stated that they (the Canaanites) made war upon them so that none of them were spared, and the Israelites were not induced to show mercy to the neglect of the commandment of God."[1] God's sovereign work of hardening the hearts of the Canaanites was done in order to effect His will for Israel.

The subject of God's hardening the heart of man is dealt with in some detail in the account of the Exodus. It is stated ten times that God hardened Pharaoh's heart; however, it also is stated ten times that Pharaoh hardened his own heart. Both concepts are true, for from a human standpoint, man is responsible and Pharaoh hardened his heart in rebellion against God; but from a divine standpoint, God actively hardened Pharaoh's heart as a judicial act. The fact that Scripture teaches both concepts does not mean it contradicts itself, but rather finite human beings must see that they cannot lay hold of the mysteries of God apart from faith. The fact that God gives men up to their sin is clearly seen in Romans 1:24, 26, 28. It is also true that God desires that the wicked should repent and live (Ezek. 33:11) and that God desires all men to come to a knowledge of the truth and be saved (1 Tim. 2:4; 2 Peter 3:9). However, as God grants His general gift of grace to fallen humanity, people respond differently, and the same sun that softens the butter also hardens the clay (Matt. 5:45).[2]

During the conquest of Canaan, Joshua fought against the Anakites, completely routing them from the land (11:22). The Anakites were descendants of Anak (cf. Num. 13:33) and are generally thought to have been giants. This is in part derived from repeated comments regarding their strength (vv. 28, 31). The fact that the Israelites saw themselves as grasshoppers in their eyes also supports this view. The term literally means "long-necked (tall) men" and is therefore under-

---

[1]Keil and Delitzsch, *Joshua, Judges, Ruth*, pp. 123–124.

[2]The sovereignty of God and the responsibility of man is one of many antinomies in the Bible. Both aspects of the discussion are true and both must be emphasized to avoid perversion. God is sovereign; yet man has genuine freedom to make choices. Boa relates an antinomy to the omniscience and omnipotence of God and concludes we must learn to live with the antinomy by accepting both truths; cf. Kenneth Boa, *God, I Don't Understand* (Wheaton, Ill: Victor Books, 1975), pp. 46–74.

stood as early giant people who lived around Hebron and in Philistia.[3]

Following Joshua's expulsion of the Anakites, the latter were relegated to the three Philistine cities of Gaza, Gath, and Ashdod (11:22). The conquest of the Anakites was significant because they caused the ten spies to bring a bad report resulting in Israel's fearing the enemy and forsaking God. This sin of unbelief resulted in that generation of Israelites wandering forty years in the desert and failing to enter the land. Joshua, however, was able to conquer the enemy and appropriate the blessings of the land because of his confidence in the Lord. His faithfulness and the resultant blessings are recorded in 11:23. Joshua received the land as an inheritance according to all that God had promised Moses (Exod. 23:29–30; Deut. 7:22).

When the three major campaigns, lasting seven years, were over, the land had rest from war (11:23). The latter statement does not mean that the warfare with the enemy was entirely over but that no more major battles were fought, for there were skirmishes in the years that followed. From Judges 1 we know that pockets of resistance remained and some cities were still unconquered. After the land was divided into the tribal allotments, it was the responsibility of the individual tribes to drive out the remaining Canaanites, but in this they utterly failed.

B. Summary of the Conquered Kings (12:1–24)

This chapter, which lists the kings that Joshua conquered, forms a logical connection with 11:23 where it is stated that Joshua "took the entire land." The names of the kings whom Joshua conquered throughout the land were not previously cited; so chapter 12 provides the names of these conquered kings. The final verse of this chapter indicates that the list totals thirty-one kings.

1. The kings east of the Jordan (12:1–6)

The opening statement of chapter 12 introduces the topic of verses 2–6—the kings that Joshua defeated on the east side of the Jordan. The extent of Israel's conquest to the east was from the Arnon Gorge to Mount Hermon. The Arnon Gorge is a natural boundary that extends from the east to the Dead Sea at its middle. Israel's conquest to the south extended to the Arabah—the Jordan Valley.[4]

---

[3]Brown, Driver, and Briggs, A Hebrew and English Lexicon of the Old Testament, p. 778.
[4]For a detailed discussion of Israel's conquest of Sihon and Og, see the comments under 2:8–14.

Israel conquered two major kings on the east side of the Jordan, Sihon and Og. Sihon reigned in Heshbon, which was situated approximately sixteen miles east of the point where the Jordan enters the Dead Sea. His territory encompassed the land from the city of Aroer (near the north rim of the Arnon Gorge) as his southern boundary to the Jabbok River in the north. His territory encompassed "half of Gilead" (12:2).

The other major king east of the Jordan whom Israel defeated was Og, king of Bashan. He was one of the Rephaites, related to the Anakites (Deut. 2:20–21). He reigned at Ashtaroth, some twenty-two miles east of the Sea of Kinnereth, and at Edrei (meaning "strength"), southeast of Ashtaroth, on the southern fork of the Yarmuk River. Edrei was a suitable defense for Og, as he could watch for invaders from the south or east from his city on the cliff. Og's territory extended northward to the land of the people of Geshur and Maacah, both nomadic tribes that dwelt near the slopes of Mount Hermon.

Moses conquered Sihon and Og (cf. Num. 21:21–35) and allocated the territory to the tribes of Reuben and Gad and to the half-tribe of Mannaseh.

2. The kings west of the Jordan (12:7–24)

a) Summary (12:7–8)

The opening statement points out that west of the Jordan Joshua conquered all the kings from Mount Halak in the south to Mount Hermon in the north (Baal Gad appears to be a synonym for Baal Hermon). Having conquered the land, Joshua gave it to the tribes of Israel as a possession (12:7). The statement anticipates the division of the land in chapters 13–22.

b) The central kings (12:9)

The thirty-one kings that Joshua identified (cf. 12:24) each represents an independent city-state, and Joshua listed them in the order in which he defeated them. Jericho was the first city taken by Israel after their march across the Jordan (6:1–27). The conquest of Ai followed (8:1–29).

c) The southern kings (12:10–16)

The kings of Jerusalem, Hebron, Jarmuth, Lachish, and Eglon represent the Amorite alliance that invaded Gibeon but was subsequently defeated by Israel (10:3–27). Gezer and Debir were previously mentioned as cities conquered in the southern campaign (10:33,

38). The following three, Geder, Hormah, and Arad, were not mentioned earlier. Geder, meaning "wall," was probably located in the western Judean slopes. Hormah, previously called Zephath, was apparently in the area of Beersheba and Ziklag. Its site is uncertain. Arad was twenty-three miles east of Beersheba. Libnah is listed earlier (10:29); Adullam was conquered in the expedition into the western foothills (cf. 15:35). Makkedah was the site to which Israel pursued the fleeing Amorite kings (10:10). Bethel, which earlier was called Luz, was the place where Jacob had his dream (Gen. 28:10–17).

d) The northern kings (12:17–24)

Tappuah was in Ephraim near the southern border of Manasseh and south of Shechem. Hepher is probably et-Tayibeh, "about ten miles west of Samaria, on the Via Maris, the Mediterranean Trunk Road used so often by the Egyptian military expeditions."[5] Aphek, identified as Ras el-Ain, lay in western Ephraim, about eight miles from the Mediterranean; later it was a Philistine base of operation against Israel (1 Sam. 4:1). Lasharon is unclear. The Septuagint reading, "the king of Aphek of Sharon," may indicate that the term actually defines Aphek.

The kings of Galilee are described in 12:19–23. Madon lies in Naphtali, immediately west of the Sea of Kinnereth. The great city of Hazor is mentioned in 11:10–15. The Septuagint indicates that Shimron Meron refers to two cities, Shimron being allied with Hazor (v. 1), and Meron being the site of Israel's battle with Hazor (v. 5). Acshaph was also allied with Hazor (v. 1). Taanach was situated southeast of Megiddo, guarding the Via Maris at the southeastern end of the Plain of Jezreel. Megiddo was also a strategic location guarding a pass through the hills; later Solomon fortified Megiddo (1 Kings 9:15). Kedesh, which lay northwest of Lake Huleh in Naphtali, later became a city of refuge (20:7). Jokneam lay just south of the Kishon River on the border of Asher and Manasseh. Dor was south of Mount Carmel along the Mediterranean Sea. Goyim, meaning "nations" or "Gentiles," may be a reference to Harosheth Haggoyim (Judg. 4:2), just north of the Kishon River on the border of Asher and Zebulun. Tirzah was northeast of Shechem in central Manasseh and may have been the northern capital for a time (cf. 1 Kings 15:21, 33).

---

[5] Rea, "Joshua," p. 221.

For Further Study

1. Why was Joshua successful (cf. 11:16, 23; 12:7–8)? How can we be assured of success in life?

2. Why did God not give Joshua an immediate, swift victory (cf. 11:18)? Why does God allow us to face serious challenges over a prolonged period of time?

3. Locate and identify the major areas of Canaan on a map (cf. 11:16).

4. Were the inhabitants of the cities responsible for their actions in view of the fact that Scripture says the Lord hardened their hearts (11:20)? Defend your conclusion.

PART THREE:
DISTRIBUTION OF THE LAND

indicate Joshua must have been near one hundred years of age when the command was given in chapter 13. The division of the land was to be completed before the death of Joshua; for this reason the apportioning needed to be effected soon.

The land that remained to be apportioned and appropriated is described in 13:2–6. It included "all the regions of the Philistines" (v. 2). This is the only mention of the Philistines in Joshua. A major influx of Philistines from Crete occurred during the twelfth century B.C. However, since the Philistines are mentioned earlier (cf. Gen. 21:32; 26:1; Exod. 13:17), it is recognized that earlier groups of Philistines settled along the coast of Canaan.[2] The Geshurites lived to the south of the Philistines, near Sinai. David raided the Geshurites while he was in exile (1 Sam. 27:8).

The "Shihor River" (13:3; NASB, "the Shihor") has been understood to be a lagoon, a part of the eastern Nile Delta.[3] Ekron was just north of Judah in Danite territory; it was the most northerly of the five Philistine cities. The Philistines are described as "rulers" (13:3; literally, "tyrants"). They occupied the five cities of Gaza, Ashdod, Ashkelon, Gath, and Ekron.

The Avvites had dwelt in the land prior to the coming of the Philistines, who apparently displaced them (cf. Deut. 2:23). Moving northward, Joshua says Israel is to appropriate the coastal Canaanite land as far "from Arah" (13:4 NASB, "and Mearah") "of the Sidonians." Gebal, a city north of Sidon on the Mediterranean, was later called Byblos by the Greeks. Israel was also to appropriate the territory of Lebanon—eastward of Gebal. Northward Israel was to claim territory to Lebo Hamath—more than one hundred miles north of Damascus on the Orontes River.

That the Lord's promise to drive out the enemy before Israel in 13:6 was conditioned by obedience is seen in Deuteronomy 11:22–23. Only as Israel would walk in harmony with her covenant relationship as rooted in the Mosaic Law would the Lord dispossess her enemies. The Book of Judges records the details of Israel's failure to do so.

Although Israel had not yet possessed all the land, God commanded Joshua to divide the entire land by lot and apportion it to the nine-and-a-half tribes (13:6–7). This was a lesson in faith for Joshua, for he had to trust the God of Israel to give the tribes what he now allotted to them.

[2]Unger, *Archaeology and the Old Testament*, pp. 90–91.
[3]Gray, *Joshua, Judges and Ruth*, p. 129.

B. Allocation to the Eastern Tribes (13:8–33)

Since the nine-and-a-half tribes were receiving their inheritance
west of the Jordan, the writer mentions the fact that Reuben, Gad, and
the half-tribe of Manasseh had already received their inheritance east
of the Jordan. The record of Moses' allocation of the land to the two-
and-a-half tribes is mentioned in Numbers 32 and Deuteronomy
3:12–17.

1. *Inheritance of the eastern tribes* (13:8–14)

The southern boundary of the eastern allotment was the Arnon
Gorge which extended westward into the Dead Sea. The city of Aroer,
on the north rim of the Arnon Gorge, helped mark the southern boundary. Dibon and Medeba were cities east of the Dead Sea and further
defined the area of Israel's eastern possession.

The eastern boundary of the allotment was the territory of the Ammonites. Northward the possession included the land of Gilead—
describing the area north and south of the Jabbok River. The extent of
the northern possession was Mount Hermon (13:11). The eastern allotment also included all the land of Og, king of Bashan (v. 12).

The statement that Israel did not dispossess the people of Geshur or
Maacah is significant, for it anticipates the failure recorded in the Book
of Judges. Israel's impending failure is mentioned several times in
Joshua (cf. 15:63; 16:10; 17:12–13) and comes to a climax in Judges 1
(cf. vv. 21, 27–30, 32–33). The chaos of Judges finds its failure in
Israel's disobedience—they failed to drive out the Canaanites according to God's command.

The reader is reminded that the tribe of Levi did not receive an
inheritance (13:14). Although Levi was one of the sons of Jacob, the
Lord was his inheritance since he represented the priestly tribe (cf.
13:33; Num. 18:20).

2. *Inheritance of Reuben* (13:15–23)

The territory of Reuben was bounded by the Dead Sea on the west,
the Arnon Gorge on the south, the Ammonite territory on the east, and
to a northern point parallel with the Amorite city of Heshbon. The
inheritance encompassed the fertile plain on the eastern plateau
(13:17f.). Reuben inherited those cities mentioned in verses 17–20 as
well as other cities within his territory that were not mentioned (v. 21).

3. Inheritance of Gad (13:24–28)

The tribe of Gad also received an inheritance east of the Jordan River. This included "the territory of Jazer" (13:25; some take Jazer to be a town in Gilead). The inheritance also included all the territory of Gilead—the land north and south of the Jabbok River—and half the Ammonite country. Specifically, the southern boundary was the city of Heshbon (v. 26); the Jordan River was the boundary on the west, while the southern shore of the Sea of Kinnereth, near the Yarmuk River, bounded Gad on the north (v. 27).

4. Inheritance of Manasseh (13:29–33)

The half-tribe of Manasseh also had its inheritance on the east side of the Jordan. It inherited Bashan, which was a fertile and fruitful land.

> Bashan was a broad, fertile plateau ranging from 1,600 to 2,300 ft. in height. It was well adapted for raising cattle (Ps 22:12; Ezek 39:18) and was celebrated for its sheep and goats (Deut 32:14), and great groves of oak trees (Isa 2:13; Ezek 27:6; Zech 11:2).[4]

Manasseh was bounded on the west by the Sea of Kinnereth and Lake Huleh, while the southern boundary ran near the Yarmuk River. It included sixty cities, along with the major cities of Ashtaroth and Edrei.

C. Allocation to the Western Tribes (14:1–19:51)

1. Inheritance by lot (14:1–5)

The general boundaries of the land were already given in Numbers 34:1–12. Within that boundary, representatives of the nine-and-a-half tribes would cast lots to determine the boundaries of the tribes. Joshua and Eleazar were to supervise the apportioning with one leader from each tribe present (Num. 34:16–29; Josh. 14:1).

Joshua explains the phrase "nine-and-a-half tribes" (14:2) in verses 3–4. The twelve sons of Jacob formed the twelve tribes of Israel; however, Levi represented the priestly tribe and did not receive an inheritance (v. 3). It would then appear that only eleven tribes received an inheritance. Joshua clarifies this in verse 4 by reminding the reader that the two sons of Joseph, Ephraim and Manasseh, actually represented two tribes because of Jacob's blessing (Gen. 48:5). While

---

[4]Huey, "Bashan," ZPEB, vol. 1, p. 486.

the Levites did not receive an inheritance in accordance with the other tribes, they were given forty-eight cities throughout the land, along with the pasture land for their livestock and as their property. Their land was to extend outward "fifteen hundred feet" (Hebrew: one thousand cubits) in every direction from the city wall (Num. 35:1–8).[5]

A number of factors were involved in dividing the land among the tribes: (1) Eleazar, Joshua, and the household leaders administered the lot (14:1). The leaders determined the boundaries. (2) The apportioning of the land was determined through lot. The practice of apportioning conquered territory was used by the Athenians and also the Romans.[6] (3) There was a consideration given to the larger tribes, providing them with a larger inheritance (Num. 26:54). This was true in some, but not all, cases. (4) The division of the land also reflected the predicted blessings of Jacob (Gen. 48–49). (5) The division of the land was enhanced by surveying the land (18:6).

Calvin clarifies the process of dividing the land:

> This was the force of the lot: there were ten lots cast in such a manner as to decide that some were to be next to the Egyptians, some to have the seacoasts, some to occupy the higher ground, and some to settle in the valleys. When this was done, it remained for the heads of the nation to determine the boundaries of their different territories according to some equitable standard. It was their place, therefore, to ascertain how many thousand heads there were in each tribe, and then to adjudicate a larger or smaller space according to the size of the tribe.[7]

2. *Inheritance of Caleb* (14:6–15)

As the division of the land was about to begin, Caleb came before Joshua, reminding him of Moses' earlier promise (14:6; cf. Deut. 1:36). Because Caleb and Joshua had responded in faith rather than discouraging the people, God was giving both of them an inheritance in the land (cf. Num. 13:30; 14:6–9). In contrast to the unbelieving ten men who spied out the land, Joshua and Caleb believed God would give them the victory. Therefore, Moses promised an inheritance in the land to Caleb, who had "followed the LORD my God wholeheartedly" (14:8).

Caleb is called "the Kenizzite" (14:6), a name that probably does not

---

[5]For a helpful discussion and illustration of the thorny interpretative problem concerning the one thousand cubits and two thousand cubits of Numbers 35:4–5, see C. F. Keil and F. Delitzsch, *The Pentateuch* in *Biblical Commentary on the Old Testament*, vol. 3 (Grand Rapids: Eerdmans, 1968 reprint), pp. 259–260.

[6]Cf. Fay, "The Book of Joshua," p. 123.

[7]Quoted by Keil and Delitzsch, *Joshua, Judges, Ruth*, p. 145.

refer to aliens or the descendants of Esau (cf. Gen. 15:19; 36:10–11). Rather, Kenaz was a Judahite from whom Caleb also descended and the name was continued in the family (cf. Judg. 1:13; 1 Chron. 4:13–15).

Caleb was eighty-five years old now (14:10), having been forty years old when Moses promised him the inheritance (v. 7). With the desert wanderings of thirty-eight years, this indicates again the conquest took seven years (40 + 38 = 78; 85 − 78 = 7). It was now the year 1399 B.C.

This passage indicates there was a direct relationship between "follow[ing] the LORD . . . wholeheartedly" (14:8) and being "as strong . . . as [in] the day Moses sent me out" (v. 11). Caleb's strength remained, for he was "just as vigorous to go out to battle now as [he] was then." The Hebrew phrase for "to go out" is used in contexts of leadership and is illustrated in the role of the shepherd (Num. 27:17; cf. Deut. 28:6; 31:2). Thus Caleb not only continued to guide the nation in war but also in leadership.

Caleb wasn't ready to retire at eighty-five, let alone sixty-five! He wanted new horizons and new battles. He didn't even look at the easy task but asked for a challenge! He requested the hill country around Hebron, located about twenty-five miles south of Jerusalem and directly west of the center of the Dead Sea. Although Hebron was only eighteen miles away, the elevation of the sea was 1300 feet below sea level while Hebron was 2800 feet above sea level. This means it was a strenuous march up to Hebron, a city located in a valley between two mountain ridges. Hebron's former name, Kiriath Arba, the city of Arba (14:15), may have originally denoted a tetrapolis, an alliance of four other cities with Hebron.

Caleb demonstrated his continuing faith by wanting to drive out the Anakites, who were related to the Nephilim. It is generally thought they were a race of giant people (Num. 13:33). The ten Israelite spies had seen themselves as grasshoppers in the sight of the Nephilim. The enemy that Caleb faced was the same enemy that caused the Israelites to falter in faith at Kadesh Barnea. Caleb revealed that at eighty-five he had not lost his faith—he was still prepared to see God provide the victory over the Anakites.

Upon receiving Caleb's request, Joshua blessed him (14:13). In the Old Testament, blessing usually denotes the bestowal of good in a material sense; hence, Joshua's blessing indicates Joshua was giving

Hebron to Caleb. The clause "[Joshua] gave him Hebron as his inheritance" explains the previous clause "Joshua blessed Caleb." Thus Caleb received Hebron as an inheritance, the reason being emphasized by the words "because he followed the LORD, the God of Israel, wholeheartedly" (v. 14).

3. *Inheritance of Judah* (15:1–63)

Judah was the kingly tribe from which the promised Messiah would come. Jacob, the father of the nation, had predicted that Judah would enjoy a place of blessing among the tribes (Gen. 49:8–12). Jacob indicated there would be a continuation of the throne-right until the Messiah would appear (Gen. 49:10; NASB, "until Shiloh comes").

a) *The southern border* (15:1–4)

Judah received a large territorial inheritance due in part, as previously mentioned, to their size (see comment on 14:2–4). Judah's population according to the new census was 76,500 men twenty years of age and older (Num. 26:22).

The southern border of Judah began at the southwestern end of the Dead Sea in the territory of Edom. The border angled southwest, reaching "to the Desert of Zin in the extreme south" (15:1). The border extended south to include Kadesh Barnea (15:3; Num. 34:4). The precise location of Zin is difficult to define; in fact, its location overlapped with the Desert of Paran. The Desert of Zin appears to have extended from the Wadi of Egypt in the west, south to Kadesh Barnea, and eastward to Scorpion (Hebrew, *Akrabbim*) Pass. From Kadesh Barnea, Judah's border followed a northwest course to the Wadi of Egypt and ended at the Mediterranean Sea. The Wadi of Egypt is the modern Wady el-'Arish that empties into the Mediterranean about fifty miles southwest of Gaza. The river marked a dividing line: eastward the land could be cultivated; southwest the land was desert.

b) *The eastern and northern borders* (15:5–11)

The eastern border of Judah was the entire western side of the Dead Sea north to where the Jordan enters that sea. From the Dead Sea the border extended several miles further north to Beth Hoglah. The border then extended westward, just south of Jerusalem. From Jerusalem the border followed a northwest course to Kiriath Jearim (15:9). From there the boundary sloped southwest to Beth Shemesh, on toward Timnah, then northwest, following the Sorek River and ending at the Mediterranean Sea.

c) *The western border* (15:12)

The coastline of the Mediterranean Sea formed the western boundary of Judah.

d) *Towns of Caleb* (15:13–19)

This section follows the thought of 14:6–15, where Caleb requested and received Hebron for an inheritance. The passage is also repeated in Judges 1:10–15. The city of Debir is also included; perhaps it was one of the cities of the tetrapolis. Caleb immediately launched his attack and rooted out three sons (i.e., three families) of Anak. Afterward, Caleb attacked Debir, which must have been a formidable foe since Caleb promised the conqueror of Debir his daughter Acsah for his wife (15:16). Caleb's younger brother, Othniel (cf. 15:17; Judg. 1:13; 3:9), conquered Debir and married Acsah. It was not forbidden by the law of Moses for a man to marry his niece as Othniel did (but Othniel also had his brother as his father-in-law!). Othniel later became the first judge of Israel.

Acsah approached her father, alighting from her donkey as the sign of a serious request. She had received land in the Negev from him but was not satisfied; she also wanted springs of water. She requested, "Do me a special favor" (15:19; Hebrew, *berakah*, denoting a "present," cf. Gen. 33:11). The explanatory statement in 15:19, "give me also springs of water," indicates the request for a tangible gift.

Caleb complied and gave his daughter "the upper and lower springs" (15:19). "The 'springs' (Heb. *gulloth*) have been associated with the ground wells at Debir (Tell Beit Mirsim) or are cisterns or reservoirs perhaps to be sought in Sel ed-Dilbe southwest of Hebron. The importance of cisterns in the Negev has been dramatically illustrated by recent explorations there."[8]

e) *Towns of Judah* (15:20–63)

The cities of Judah are grouped according to region: the Negev (vv. 21–32), the western foothills (vv. 33–47), the hill country (vv. 48–60), and the desert (vv. 61–62).

While Joshua defeated the king of Jerusalem, the city remained in the hands of the Jebusites (cf. 10:5ff.). The residential area of Jerusalem was later conquered, but the city was never completely subjugated until David conquered Jerusalem (cf. Judg. 1:8, 21; 2 Sam. 5:6–7).

---

[8]May, "Joshua," p. 299.

4. *Inheritance of Ephraim* (16:1-10)

a) *The southern border of Ephraim* (16:1-4)

The territory for the sons of Joseph was drawn as one lot (16:1-4), and the territory was divided among Ephraim and Manasseh later (16:5-17:11). Thus chapters 16-17 form a unit. Although Joseph was one of the sons of Jacob, two sons of Joseph, Ephraim and Manasseh, received the inheritance; thus Joseph received a double blessing (cf. Gen. 49:22). Ephraim's inheritance is mentioned first because he received priority in the blessing over his brother, Manasseh (Gen. 48:14).

The southern boundary of the inheritance of the sons of Joseph is given in 16:1-4. The major part of the boundary became the southern border of Ephraim. This is seen in the phrase "ending at the sea" (v. 3) that must describe a portion of Manasseh's southwestern border since Ephraim did not front toward the sea. The southern border of Ephraim began at the Jordan River and extended west through Jericho and Ai; at Bethel the border turned south and then went westward to Beth Horon. Gezer, which guarded the entrance to the Valley of Aijalon from the coastal plain, marked the southwesterly point of Ephraim. From there the boundary turned north to the Kanah Ravine and then followed the ravine to the Mediterranean Sea. The last segment formed part of the southern boundary of Manasseh.

b) *The territory of Ephraim* (16:5-9)

A brief description of the southern boundary is given in 16:5 but stated in more detail in verses 1-3. The writer assumes a central point, Micmethath, in describing the northern border of Ephraim. In verses 6-7 he looks eastward in describing the Ephraimite border. The border reached to Taanath Shiloh, the most northerly point of Ephraim, then proceeded southeast to Ataroth near the Jordan River. Finally, the border turned south to include Naarah and Jericho. It appears that Ephraim also assumed the territory eastward of these three cities to the Jordan River.

In 16:8 the border continued westward from the central point of Tappuah, following a course to the Kanah Ravine and ending at the sea. From this description it appears that Ephraim may have had an outlet on the Mediterranean Sea.[9]

---

[9]That the tribal boundaries are difficult to establish is clear in consulting various sources. A number of them have Ephraim bordering the Mediterranean; cf. Aharoni and Avi-Yonah, *The Macmillan Bible Atlas,* p. 52; George Ernest Wright and Floyd Vivian Filson, *The Westminster Historical Atlas to the Bible* (Philadelphia: Westminster Press,

c) *The failure of Ephraim* (16:10)

Ephraim failed to drive out the Canaanites from Gezer. This failure is a continuing emphasis in these chapters, and the failure of Ephraim anticipates the Book of Judges (see comment on 13:13). While Israel was victorious in a military sense over the Canaanites, they failed to rid the land of them; instead, Israel reduced the Canaanites to forced labor (16:10). This was similar to Solomon's corvée that he used in his building projects (1 Kings 9:21). Israel's refusal to totally exterminate the Canaanites was contrary to God's command (cf. Deut. 7:2) and resulted in a series of divine judgments during the chaotic period of the judges.

5. *Inheritance of Manasseh* (17:1–18)

In defining Manasseh's inheritance, attention is drawn to Manasseh's being "Joseph's firstborn" (17:1; Gen. 41:51; 48:14). This explains the twofold inheritance of Joseph—one on the east side of the Jordan and another on the west side.

a) *Family of Manasseh* (17:1–6)

Makir, the firstborn of Manasseh (Gen. 50:23), received Gilead and Bashan east of the Jordan as his inheritance. This territory had been previously allotted to the Makirites by Moses (Num. 32:39–40). The name Makir does not denote an individual, but the descendants of Makir. The inheritance was based on the fact that the Makirites were great soldiers.

The other descendants of Manasseh received an inheritance west of the Jordan bordering Ephraim. The six sons of Manasseh whose families inherited the western territory were Abiezer, Helek, Asriel, Shechem, Hepher, and Shemida. However, Zelophehad, the son of Hepher, had no male descendants, only five daughters. The five came to Moses and Eleazar with their request for an inheritance. Moses granted their request and Manasseh's final inheritance west of the Jordan was divided between five sons and five descendant daughters (17:3–6; cf. Num. 27:1–11).

b) *Territory of Manasseh* (17:7–11)

The northern boundary of Manasseh stretched to the river or stream called Shihor Libnath (19:26), just south of Dor, while Micmethath,

---

1956), p. 42; Aharoni, *The Land of the Bible*, p. 229. Yet in contrast to the others, Aharoni terminates Ephraim's eastern boundary short of the Jordan River. Others do not give Ephraim a Mediterranean outlet; cf. Wood, *A Survey of Israel's History*, p. 186; Jensen, *Joshua: Rest-Land Won*, p. 112.

just east of Shechem, was the south-central boundary (17:7). From Micmethath, the boundary proceeded southward to En Tappuah. From there the boundary followed the Kanah Ravine to the Mediterranean Sea. The northern boundary is stated in nebulous terms, with Manasseh bordering Asher in the northwest and Issachar in the northeast. In addition, Manasseh received six cities (17:11) within the territory of Asher and Issachar.

   c) *Failure of Manasseh* (17:12–13)

While Manasseh extended his territory into Asher and Issachar, the Canaanites in these cities could not be subdued. Later, when the Manassehites became strong, they subjected the Canaanites to forced labor (cf. Judg. 1:27–29).

   d) *Complaint of Manasseh* (17:14–18)

The sons of Joseph (i.e., Ephraim and Manasseh) came to Joshua, complaining that their inheritance was small in proportion to their population. The complaint was unjustified, since Ephraim (32,500; Num. 26:37) and half of Manasseh (26,350; v. 34) numbered less than either Judah (76,500; v. 22) or Issachar (64,300; v. 25)—the latter having far less territory. Furthermore, the central hill country of Ephraim was a lush, fertile area.

Joshua portrayed wisdom, leadership, and faith in his response (17:15). He commanded the descendants of Joseph to go up to the forested hill country in the central ridge of the land and clear the land.[10] Joshua's answer indicates that while these tribes had received an allotment, they had not appropriated it. Once more, however, the two tribes expressed dissatisfaction, indicating a lack of faith. They complained of the iron chariots of the Canaanites although God had earlier promised to give them victory in precisely that situation (Deut. 20:1). Ephraim and Manasseh saw the Canaanites as superior militarily in possessing the chariots of iron and superior territorially in possessing the important Valley of Jezreel.

Joshua repeated his earlier response in an amplified way. He exhorted them to take courage and to go up and possess the land. He

---

[10]Aharoni indicates the historical importance of Israel's possessing the hill country: "The Israelite occupation brought about a fundamental change. Now the hilly regions also became densely populated, and most of the spaces formerly left open between the various regions were filled. For the first time in the history of the country the centre of population actually moved into the hill country; and when the Israelite tribes grew in strength and completed their domination of the plains, the conditions necessary for uniting the land into one political and ethnic unit were established" (Aharoni, *The Land of the Bible*, p. 220).

assured them that their numerical strength and great power were enough to defeat the enemy!

6. *Inheritance of the seven tribes* (18:1–19:48)

a) *Installation of the tabernacle* (18:1)

With Israel's settlement in the land, a permanent location for the tabernacle became essential. The initial site of Shiloh, meaning "place of rest," was located in the central hill country of Ephraim, just south of Shechem and Mount Gerizim. It is uncertain why Shiloh was chosen. Perhaps "the fact that it was seemingly uninhabited in Canaanite times . . . suggested it as an 'uncontaminated' location for worship."[11]

God had determined where the tabernacle was to be set up (Deut. 12:11). The name designation for the first location of the tabernacle is significant and suggests "rest" until the promised Messiah would come (Gen. 49:10). The tabernacle remained at Shiloh until the Battle of Aphek (*c.* 1075 B.C.) when the Philistines captured the ark (1 Sam. 4:1ff.). In David's day the tabernacle apparently was set up at Nob (cf. 1 Sam. 21:1–6), and afterward, having captured Jerusalem, he brought the tabernacle there to the ultimate place of worship.

b) *Instruction to the seven tribes* (18:2–10)

1) *Investigation of the land* (18:2–7)

Seven tribes still had not appropriated the land that God had given them, that is, they had not divided the land by lot to define their borders and had not defeated the remaining enemies in the land. Admonishing them for their failure, Joshua instructed them to send out another mission, with three men going from each of the seven tribes. The purpose was for

> preparation of lists of the towns in the different parts of the land, with an account of their size and character; also with "notices of the quality and condition of the soil; what lands were fertile, and what they produced; where the country was mountainous, and where it was level; which lands were well watered, and which were dry; and any other things that would indicate the character of the soil, and facilitate a comparison between the different parts of the land."[12]

The territories of Judah, Ephraim, and Manasseh had already been established. When the men returned with the needed information,

---

[11]Andersen, "Shiloh," ZPEB, vol. 5, p. 402.
[12]Keil and Delitzsch, *Joshua, Judges, Ruth*, pp. 186–187.

Joshua would divide the remaining land into seven portions for the tribes that were to receive their inheritance west of the Jordan.

2) *Division of the land* (18:8–10)

The men obeyed Joshua's command to go map out the land. They wrote a seven-part description on a scroll—probably for the purpose of casting lots for the seven tribes. The duration of the sojourn is not stated, but the suggestions of seven months by Josephus and seven years by the rabbis are without warrant. When the men returned to Joshua, he cast lots for them in Shiloh before the Lord. The phrase "in the presence of the LORD" (18:10) indicates the event took place at the tabernacle, the place of the Lord's presence among Israel (cf. 19:51).

c) *Inheritance of Benjamin* (18:11–28)

1) *Territory of Benjamin* (18:11–20)

Although the territory of Benjamin was very small, it was nonetheless also very significant. Sandwiched between the two rivals, Judah and Ephraim, Benjamin served as a buffer. By its central location, Benjamin also served as a unifying influence among the tribes—particularly since Jerusalem fell within its boundaries. It is also noteworthy that Benjamin was situated next to Ephraim since Benjamin and Joseph (father of Ephraim) were both sons of Rachel (Gen. 30:22–24; 35:18).

The northern border of Benjamin coincided with the southern border of Ephraim. From the Jordan River the boundary between the two tribes followed a westward course to Jericho and on to Luz (Bethel) where it turned southwestward and touched Kiriath Jearim. The southern border of Benjamin coincided with the northern border of Judah. From Kiriath Jearim the border extended southeast to encompass the southern slope of Jerusalem; then the border proceeded northeastward to Beth Hoglah, where it turned south and ended at the Dead Sea. The Jordan River formed the eastern border.

2) *Towns of Benjamin* (18:21–28)

The towns of Benjamin fall into two groups. The first group contains twelve towns and pertains to the eastern part of the territory (18:21–24). The second group includes fourteen towns and pertains to those towns situated in the western part of the tribal territory (18:25–28).

d) *Inheritance of Simeon* (19:1–9)

1) *Towns of Simeon* (19:1–8)

The tribe of Simeon did not receive its own territory but rather fell within the territory of Judah. This was in fulfillment of the curse uttered by Jacob in which he indicated that both Simeon and Levi would be dispersed and scattered in the land of Israel (Gen. 49:7).

The towns of Simeon are divided into two groups, the first consisting of thirteen located in the Negev (19:2–6; some authorities find fourteen towns, reading Beersheba and Sheba in verse 2 as two towns, cf. NASB, RSV, KJV). The second group had four towns (19:7) with two in the Negev and two in the western foothills.

2) *Share from Judah* (19:9)

This explanatory verse indicates that the original allotment to Judah was too large for them, so Simeon shared in the inheritance of Judah.

e) *Inheritance of Zebulun* (19:10–16)

1) *Territory of Zebulun* (19:10–14)

Zebulun received a small inheritance in the Lower Galilee region in the central portion of the country, midway between the Sea of Galilee and the Mediterranean Sea. Nazareth would later be in its territory.

> Divine wisdom placed the Leah tribes, Zebulun and Issachar, to the north of the Rachel tribes in order to cement the union of all Israel. Judah, Issachar, and Zebulun encamped together in the wilderness (Num. 23:3–7; 10:14–16). These ties persisted for centuries. Mary and Joseph, for instance, both of the tribe of Judah, dwelt in the old territory of Zebulun.[13]

2) *Towns of Zebulun* (19:15–16)

The inheritance of Zebulun included twelve towns of which only five are mentioned here.

f) *Inheritance of Issachar* (19:17–23)

1) *Towns of Issachar* (19:17–21)

The territory of Issachar extended beyond Jezreel and included sixteen towns and their villages.

2) *Territory of Issachar* (19:22–23)

A definitive description of Issachar's territory is not given. Issachar was bounded on the south by Manasseh and shared the fertile Plain of Jezreel (Greek, Esdraelon) with Zebulun on the west. Naphtali bounded Issachar on the north and the Jordan River on the east.

g) *Inheritance of Asher* (19:24–31)

1) *Territory of Asher* (19:24–29)

Asher enjoyed a lengthy coastal area along the Mediterranean Sea. It extended from Shihor Lipnah (below Mount Carmel) in the south to Tyre and Sidon in the north (a territory they did not fully appropriate).

---

[13]Rea, "Joshua," p. 226.

2) *Towns of Asher* (19:30-31)

The territory of Asher inherited twenty-two towns and their villages.

h) *Inheritance of Naphtali* (19:32-39)

1) *Territory of Naphtali* (19:32-34)

On the east, Naphtali was bounded by the Sea of Kinnereth, the Jordan, and Lake Huleh. Issachar and Zebulun formed its southern boundary, and Asher bounded it on the west.

2) *Towns of Naphtali* (19:35-39)

Naphtali inherited nineteen towns, one the great city of Hazor.

i) *Inheritance of Dan* (19:40-48)

1) *Territory of Dan* (19:40-46)

Dan inherited a small but fruitful territory between Ephraim and Judah. The inheritance lay in the western foothills just south of the Plain of Sharon. It was bounded on the east by Benjamin and on the west by the Mediterranean Sea.

2) *Possession of Dan* (19:47-48)

After Joshua's death the Danites found their territory was too small due to the presence of Amorites on the plain. Hence some Danites migrated to the north and conquered an area east of Naphtali. Here these apostate Danites captured the town of Leshem (Laish) and renamed it Dan.

j) *Inheritance of Joshua* (19:49-51)

At the conclusion of the division, the tribes gave Joshua the town of Timnath Serah as his inheritance. The town was eleven miles southwest of Shiloh in the central hill country of Ephraim. The inheritance was given "as the LORD had commanded" (19:50). No other mention is made of this command in the Pentateuch, but perhaps it was given at the time Caleb received the promise of his inheritance.

For Further Study

1. Study Genesis 49. How does this chapter relate to the inheritance of the tribes of Israel?

2. Why did Israel fail to drive out the Canaanites from the land when God had promised to give them the land?

3. Study a Bible atlas on the conquest of the land.

4. What was the place of Levi in the inheritance?

5. Study the unusual qualities of Caleb in his old age (14:6-15).

6. What important place did the tribe of Judah have in the nation Israel? Read a Bible dictionary or encyclopedia article for clarification.

Chapter 11

Allocation of Towns
(Joshua 20:1–22:34)

A. Cities of Refuge (20:1–9)

1. *Reiteration for the provision* (20:1–6)

In order to protect a person guilty of unintentional killing from the avenger of blood, God established six cities of refuge in the land. Three were east of the Jordan; three were on the west side. The appointment of cities of refuge had previously been given to Moses (20:2). Numbers 35:6–34 provides a detailed explanation concerning those protected or unprotected by the cities of refuge. Deuteronomy 4:41–43 defines the three eastern cities, and 19:1–13 gives a further explanation through Moses.

Someone who killed another person accidentally and unintentionally was permitted to flee to a designated city of refuge. Such an act fell under the category of unintentional sins (Num. 15:22–31), and so the guilty party was allowed to live. The unpremeditated sin stands in contrast to the defiant sin that was punishable by death (vv. 30–31).

Before the one accused of murder could take up residence in a city of refuge, he would state his case before the elders of the city. Apparently the elders would first determine the validity of his claim and then admit him to their city. The city would then be obligated to protect the accused from the avenger of blood because the killing had been unpremeditated (20:5).

The accused was obligated to remain in the city of refuge until he stood trial and until the death of the high priest. Should he leave the city prior to the ruling high priest's death, he would expose himself to possible death by the blood avenger (Num. 35:25–28).

CITIES OF REFUGE

KEDESH •

Sea of Galilee

• GOLAN

RAMOTH •

SHECHEM •

BEZER •

Dead Sea

HEBRON •

The high priest's death has significance from the standpoint of Bible typology. The death of the high priest is seen as a type of the expiatory death of Christ. With the high priest's death, the accused was set free concerning his unintentional sin; with the death of Christ redemption has been provided, bringing release from the bondage of sin.

The Old Testament is explicit concerning what was required when a killing took place: (1) A murder was to be avenged by the nearest relative of the dead person. The murderer was to be put to death (Deut. 19:12; cf. Gen. 9:6; Lev. 24:21). The avenger was the *goel,* the kinsman-redeemer. (2) An unintentional killing (manslaughter) was not to be avenged, and the six cities of refuge in the land were provided as havens for those who killed unintentionally.

2. *Location of the cities of refuge* (20:7–9)

a) *The western cities of refuge* (20:7)

The cities of refuge were spread throughout the land for the benefit of the people. The first three cities listed were located west of the Jordan River. Kedesh, the northern city, was located about five miles northwest of Lake Huleh. Shechem was in the central part of the land, about midway between the Sea of Kinnereth and the Dead Sea and almost midway between the Jordan River and the Mediterranean Sea. Hebron was approximately twenty miles west of the Dead Sea.

b) *The eastern cities of refuge* (20:8–9)

The three cities east of the Jordan were Bezer, Ramoth, and Golan. Bezer was about twenty-two miles east of the northern tip of the Dead Sea. Golan was about twenty miles directly east of the Sea of Kinnereth. Ramoth was south-southeast of Golan.

B. Towns of the Levites (21:1–42)

Because the Levites were the priestly tribe, they did not receive a land inheritance; instead, God was their inheritance. However, Moses had promised them towns in which they would live, and they also would have the surrounding area as pasture land for their animals (Num. 35:2–5; Josh. 13:33).

1. *Instruction concerning the towns* (21:1–8)

Following the allocation of the cities of refuge, the Levites came forward to receive their inheritance—the towns sprinkled throughout the land. There was a distinct purpose in scattering the Levites throughout the land in the forty-eight towns. The Levites were to instruct the people; this was God's unique methodology for ensuring the dissemination of the Word of God throughout the land.

The descendants of Levi were divided into three branches, the Kohathites, the Gershonites, and the Merarites (cf. Num. 3:17; Exod. 6:16–19). The Kohathites represented the priestly line, some of them descending through Aaron. The Gershonites and Merarites represented the nonpriestly Levites and were actually subordinate to the priests. Hence, it may be said that all three branches were Levites, but only the Kohathites were priests. The Levites were actually assistants of the priests, helping them in rituals of worship and taking care of the other manual duties. The Kohathites who descended through Aaron received thirteen towns in Judah, Simeon, and Benjamin (21:4). The providence of God is clearly seen since the Aaronic Kohathites would be ministering in the temple that would ultimately be established in Jerusalem. The Kohathites that were not descendents of Aaron received ten towns in Ephraim, Dan, and the western half of the tribe of Manasseh (21:5; cf. Exod. 6:18–20). The Gershonites received thirteen towns in Issachar, Asher, Naphtali and the eastern half of the tribe of Manasseh (21:6). The Merarites received twelve towns in the territory of Reuben, Gad, and Zebulun (21:7).

2. *Allocation of the towns* (21:9–42)

a) *Allocation to the Kohathites* (21:9–26)
The descendants of Aaron received the thirteen towns mentioned in 21:9–19. The other Kohathites received the ten towns enumerated in verses 20–26.

b) *Allocation to the Gershonites* (21:27–33)
The Gershonites received two towns in the half-tribe of Manasseh, four in Issachar, four in Asher, and three in Naphtali.

c) *Allocation to the Merarites* (21:34–40)
The Merarites received four towns in Zebulun, four in Reuben, and four in the territory of Gad.

d) *Allocation to all the Levites* (21:41–42)
The Levites received as an inheritance forty-eight towns.

C. Conclusion of the Conquest (21:43–45)
This conclusion to the book is noteworthy since it bears witness to the faithfulness of the Lord: (1) The promise concerning the land was

fulfilled (1:2, 5–9). (2) The promise of rest was fulfilled (Deut. 12:9–10). While not all the enemies of the land had been exterminated, nonetheless the enemy had been militarily subjugated; in that sense, the nation enjoyed rest from their enemies. (3) The promise of conquest over their enemies had been fulfilled (1:5).

D. Contention Concerning the Altar (22:1–34)

1. Admonition (22:1–6)

The tribes of Ephraim, Gad, and Manasseh had received permission from Moses to appropriate the land east of the Jordan (Num. 32:1–42); however, they could only take possession of the land after they had helped their brothers conquer the inhabitants of the land west of the Jordan. That work had now been completed. The "then" of 22:1 refers to the completion of the conquest. Now the two-and-a-half tribes were free to return to their settlements east of the Jordan.

Joshua commended the eastern tribes for they had fulfilled their obligation (22:2–3; cf. Num. 32:20–32). The term "rest" in 22:4 refers to the completion of the conquest of the land and reflects the fulfillment of 1:15. Since the western tribes had conquered the inhabitants, the eastern tribes were free to return to their "homes" (22:4; literally, "tents"—an ancient expression for returning home, cf. Deut. 5:30; 16:7). This was important since their families had remained behind on the eastern side of the Jordan (Num. 32:17).

Following his commendation, Joshua exhorted the eastern tribes to faithfully adhere to the law (22:5). The sixfold injunction of Joshua was based on Moses' earlier words to Israel: (1) to observe the commandment and the law; (2) to love the Lord; (3) to walk in all His ways; (4) to keep His commandments; (5) to hold fast to Him; (6) to serve Him (cf. Deut. 4:4, 29; 5:10; 6:5; 10:12; 11:13, 22). This appeal was based on Israel's relationship to the Lord and the focal point of their monotheistic belief. The great statement of Deuteronomy 6:4–9, termed the "Shema," related to Israel's "hearing" and heeding the law of the Lord.[1] The injunction was important since the eastern tribes would be separated from their western brothers by the Jordan River. The Jordan Rift Valley formed a natural division of the land and hindered the unity of the twelve tribes—as this chapter aptly reveals.

---

[1]Cf. Payne, *Theology of the Older Testament*, pp. 125–127; P. C. Craigie, *The Book of Deuteronomy* in *The New International Commentary on the Old Testament* (Grand Rapids: Eerdmans, 1976), pp. 168–171.

2. Provocation (22:7-10)

Joshua sent the two-and-a-half tribes to their home on the east side of the Jordan, providing them with the spoils of war that were to be shared with those at home (Num. 31:27). The eastern tribes left Shiloh, the site of the tabernacle of the Lord (18:1), and started toward "Gilead, their own land" (22:9). In the present context the expression "Gilead, their own land" stands in contrast to "the land of Canaan" (22:10), which denotes the land west of the Jordan, while the former signifies the territory east of the Jordan.

When the eastern tribes arrived at the Jordan River, they built a large altar. It was high and broad, so as to be able to be seen from a great distance. The tribes failed to see anything wrong with this action since Moses had also built an altar to commemorate his victory over the Amalekites (Exod. 17:15). The indication is that the altar was built in the Ghor, or Jordan depression, just west of the river. The tribes who built the altar did not intend to offer sacrifices on it, but, of course, the western tribes did not know this (22:22-27).

3. Mobilization (22:11-20)

The act of the two-and-a-half tribes greatly disturbed the western tribes. The construction of the altar appeared to be a presumptuous act to the others since God had established Shiloh as the central worship center where the tabernacle now stood (18:1). The men from all the tribes were obligated to go up to Shiloh to worship three times a year (Exod. 23:17). Sacrifices were to take place only at the place appointed by the Lord (Lev. 17:8-9; Deut. 12:4-5). Thus the western tribes saw the building of the altar as an act of rebellion. A central shrine was also important since it would serve to unite the tribes of Israel and avoid fragmentation. The western tribes decided to go to war against their eastern brothers.

Phinehas, the son of Eleazar the priest, along with ten chief men from the ten tribes, came and confronted the eastern tribes with their deed. Phinehas had previously led a holy war against the Midianites (Num. 31). He carried the spiritual authority of the high priestly family in confronting the tribes.

Phinehas asked the eastern tribes how they could "break faith" with God (22:16; the same Hebrew word is used to describe a wife who has been unfaithful to her husband, Num. 5:12, 27). The sons of Israel regarded their eastern brothers as having committed spiritual adultery against their God. The unfaithful act is clearly defined in the rest of verse 16: they had turned from the Lord by building an altar and rebelling against Him (22:16).

Phinehas accused the eastern tribes of rebellion and warned them of the consequences, citing two illustrations from history of how God judged rebellion. In the first illustration, the eastern tribes were reminded of the occasion when Israel worshiped Peor, the fertility god (Num. 25), involving the nation in the licentious practices of the fertility god. On that occasion twenty-four thousand died under the judgment of God. In the rebuke there is an emphasis on rebellion against God (22:18–19). Their rebellion was committed through building an altar "other" than the altar of the Lord. The accusation is that they had built an altar in addition to the appointed altar at Shiloh. As a result of this rebellious act, they could expect a divine judgment similar to what fell at Peor.

The second illustration of warning related to the sin of Achan (22:20). Achan had acted unfaithfully concerning devoted things, and for his unfaithfulness he had perished under the judgment of God. However, Achan did not perish alone because of his sin, but about thirty-six men had perished in Israel's futile attempt to take Ai (7:1–5), and later Achan's entire family was judged (v. 24). The suggestion was that if by the sin of one man (Achan) quite a number of people were judged, how many people could they expect to be judged in this case, since *many* were involved in this rebellious act?

4. *Explanation* (22:21–29)

The response must have been immediate, and their appeal was to the sovereign knowledge of God. In their appeal to God they swore with an oath that their intentions were pure. The solemnity of their statement is seen in their threefold address of God: "The Mighty One (El), God (Elohim), the LORD (Yahweh)!" (22:22). The threefold address to God was repeated a second time. "El" denotes God as strength, power and authority; He is the strong one. The plural "Elohim" portrays God as being above all other gods. "Yahweh" comes from the verb "to be" (Exod. 3:13–15) and is the name denoting the covenant relationship of God with His people Israel.[2]

---

[2]For a helpful study of the various names as well as the combinations of the names of God, see H. B. Kuhn, "God, Names of," ZPEB, vol. 2, pp. 760–766.

The negative statement is given in 22:22–23 where the tribes suggest they did not construct the altar to offer sacrifices on it; if that was their motive in building the altar, then may God "call us to account" (cf. Deut. 18:19). By an oath they call for God's judgment if they are not speaking the truth.

Verses 24–28 provide the positive explanation concerning their purpose in building the altar. Their concern was for the unity of the twelve tribes. They feared the day when those dwelling west of the Jordan would not consider those living east of the Jordan as belonging to Israel and actually having an inheritance in the land. Therefore, they built the altar as a witness to the western tribes that they who lived east of the Jordan also had an inheritance in the land (v. 27). This altar was not to be used as a place of sacrifice, but only as a memorial that reminded the twelve tribes of their unity under Yahweh. A corroborating statement affirms that the altar was a "replica" of the altar at Shiloh (v. 28).

Thus the tribes disassociated themselves from any intended rebellion through constructing the altar.

5. Satisfaction (22:30–34)

Phinehas and the ten tribal representatives were satisfied with the explanation, for it was evident to them that the Lord was working in their midst both to prevent the apostasy of the eastern tribes and to prevent the war between the tribes.

When the delegation brought their report back to the western tribes, the Israelites rejoiced and refrained from going to war with their brothers. The altar was named "WITNESS" in accordance with their explanation (22:34; cf. vv. 27–28).

For Further Study

1. In a Bible dictionary or encyclopedia, look up various names of God and study them.

2. What principles for missions and ministry are to be drawn from the fact that the cities of the Levites were spread throughout the land?

3. Distinguish between the Old Testament teachings on murder and manslaughter and discuss the penalties for each.

4. Discuss the faithfulness of God in the light of His provision of the cities of refuge and the Levitical cities for the nation Israel.

5. Were the eastern tribes wise in building the altar? What was the value? the disadvantage?

PART FOUR: CONCLUSION

Chapter 12

Joshua's First Address: Separation
(Joshua 23:1–16)

Following the division of the land, Joshua settled in Timnath Serah, his inheritance in the hill country of Ephraim (19:50). When he realized his death was approaching, he called the Israelites together for some final words. Joshua must have been close to one hundred and ten years of age at this time (cf. 24:29). His exhortation involved two messages, a negative word and a positive statement. Remembering the Lord's instruction to him (1:8), Joshua warned the Israelites to adhere to the law of God. He reminded them of the snare that intermarriage with the heathen would bring (chap. 23). In his positive statement Joshua challenged the Israelites to serve the Lord faithfully (chap. 24).

A. Introduction (23:1–2)

The clause "After a long time had passed" modifies the following clause, "and the LORD had given Israel rest." It could read, "After many days, after the Lord had given rest to Israel."[1] This suggests a lengthy interval between the conquest of the land and Joshua's summons to Israel at the end of his life.

Although Joshua dwelt at Timnath Serah, the summons was probably to Shiloh, the location of the central sanctuary. Joshua called for "all Israel," explained as "their elders, leaders, judges, and officials" (23:2). This is not to be understood as four differing categories, for the "elders" were all the representatives of the people. The "leaders" came from the tribes, families, and fathers' houses, and from them were chosen the judges and officers of the people.[2]

---

[1]Fay, "Book of Joshua," p. 179.
[2]Keil and Delitzsch, *Joshua, Judges, Ruth*, p. 223.

B. Recollection (23:3–5)

Joshua reminded them that they had seen all that the Lord had done for them in the past. They had observed God going before them and providing them with victory over thirty-one independent city-states (23:3; cf. 12:24). Following the conquest, Joshua had divided up the land as their inheritance according to the command of the Lord (23:4, cf. 13:6–7). Now the tribes needed to appropriate the land by trusting the Lord to drive out the remaining inhabitants (23:5).

C. Exhortation (23:6–11)

The foundation of Israel's obedience and ultimate blessing rested in adherence to the law of Moses (23:6). The exhortation of Joshua to the leaders of Israel was similar to the injunction of the Lord to Joshua (1:7–8). A primary tenet of the law of Moses was separation from the Canaanites; this became a major emphasis of Joshua's address (23:7).

The warning to disassociate themselves from the nations had practical ramifications; it was designed to keep Israel from falling into idolatry. The fourfold warning concerning the foreign gods emphasizes this prohibition. (1) They were not to call on the foreign gods by name, for to do so would be to admit their reality and presence (cf. Exod. 23:13).[3] (2) They were not to swear by them, for to do so was to appeal to these gods through an oath concerning the truthfulness of a statement. (3) They were not to serve them by offering sacrifices to them. (4) They were not to bow down to them in worship. These four elements constituted an expression of worship (Deut. 6:13; 10:20); Israel was forbidden to give the allegiance of worship to the foreign Canaanite gods.

In contrast to separation from the heathen gods, Israel was to "hold fast" to the Lord (23:8). The term "hold fast" is a figure of speech that denotes the close, spiritual relationship the Israelites were to have with their God. The term is used to describe the close relationship of husband and wife (Gen. 2:24). The term "hold fast" emphasizes the loyalty that Israel was to maintain toward the Lord.

In 23:9–10 Joshua suggests why the nation was to cling to the Lord. He had conquered the nations on their behalf, allowing none to resist their onslaught. To illustrate Israel's conquest over her enemies through the help of the Lord, Joshua employs a hyperbole, stating,

---

[3]Gray, *Joshua, Judges and Ruth*, p. 189.

"One of you routs a thousand" (23:10; cf. Deut. 32:30). Joshua then returned to a familiar theme by exhorting them to love the Lord (23:11).

D. Admonition (23:12-13)

Should the Israelites disregard this word and intermarry with the heathen, they could no longer expect the Lord to lead them to victory in battle; instead, the heathen would ensnare them and cause their downfall (23:12-13). The warning is expressive, for the nations would be "snares," "traps," "whips," and "thorns" to them. All these terms depict suffering. The term "trap" refers to a device in which a bird is caught (Amos 3:5). The first two terms indicate Israel would be ensnared and led into idolatry; the last two terms indicate that the nations would be a constant source of trouble to them.[4] Ultimately, Israel would no longer possess the good land that the Lord had given them but would go into captivity ("perish from this good land").

E. Conclusion (23:14-16)

In Joshua's concluding statement, he summarized his words by reminding Israel of the certainty that all of God's words would be fulfilled. Every blessing that He had promised them had come to pass; but should they reject His word in disobedience, all the threats that He had pronounced would come to pass. God dealt with Israel on the basis that obedience would bring blessing, while disobedience would bring chastisement (cf. Lev. 26:14-33; Deut. 28:15-68).

For Further Study

1. How consistent was Joshua in obeying the word of the Lord (cf. 1:8 with 23:6)? Trace specific events and examples in the book.

2. Why is it important for the believer to continually remember the Lord's faithfulness in past events?

3. How does the statement concerning separation from the nations (23:7) relate to the Christian's relationship with unbelievers (cf. 2 Cor. 6:14-18; 2 Thess. 3:6; 2 Tim. 3:5)?

4. Analyze Deuteronomy 28 and categorize the general areas of blessing and chastisement.

---

[4]Bright, "Joshua," p. 665.

Chapter 13

Joshua's Second Address: Service
(Joshua 24:1–28)

In his final address to the nation, Joshua called for all the tribes of Israel to gather at Shechem (23:2).

A. Preamble (24:1)

Joshua called the nation together to reaffirm and renew the covenant of Israel with the Lord. The format follows the suzerainty-vassal covenant of ancient secular history. It is a bilateral treaty in which the king (the suzerain) announces his promised blessings and provisions on his vassals or subjects. The vassals, on the other hand, are obligated to fulfill certain conditions of faithfulness to their king in order to receive his provision of blessing. The suzerainty-vassal treaty was common in the ancient Near East.[1]

B. Historical Prologue: God's Provision (24:2–13)

In the prologue of the suzerainty-vassal treaty, the speaker enumerated the specific benevolent acts of the king on behalf of his subjects.[2] In this account there is a vigorous emphasis on the specific acts wherein the Lord demonstrated His faithful provision for the nation

---

[1]See Meredith G. Kline, *Treaty of the Great King* (Grand Rapids: Eerdmans, 1963) and George E. Mendenhall, *Law and Covenant in Israel and the Near East* (Pittsburgh: The Biblical Colloquium, 1955).

[2]Kline states, "Following the preamble in the international suzerainty treaties there was an historical section, written in an I-thou style, which surveyed the previous relationships of lord and vassal. Its purpose was to establish the historical justification for the lord's continuing reign. Benefits allegedly conferred by the lord upon the vassal were cited with a view to grounding the vassal's allegiance in a sense of gratitude complementary to the sense of fear which the preamble's grandiose identification of the suzerain had been calculated to inspire" (Kline, *Treaty of the Great King*, p. 52).

from its infant beginning: "I took (24:3) . . . (I) led (v. 3) . . . (I) gave (v. 4) . . . I sent (v. 5) . . . I afflicted (v. 5) . . . I did (v. 5) . . . I brought (v. 6) . . . (I) put (v. 7) . . . I did (v. 7) . . . I brought (v. 8) . . . I gave (v. 8) . . . I destroyed (v. 8) . . . I delivered (v. 10) . . . I gave (v. 11) . . . I sent (v. 12) . . . I gave (v. 13).

Joshua narrates the Lord's provision by beginning with God's founding of the nation by calling Abraham from Ur at the Euphrates River. The Lord brought Abraham into the land that He had promised him; this land was to be the land of blessing for Abraham and his posterity. God then gave Isaac and Jacob, but Jacob went down to Egypt where the nation suffered. But God continued to reveal His faithfulness by raising up Moses and bringing the Israelites out of Egypt. He delivered the Amorites into their hands; He even had Balaam bless Israel when he had intended to curse the nation. When Israel reached the land, God gave their enemies into their hand. The enemies were conquered by the Lord, who sent "the hornet" before them (24:12). Earlier prophecies had mentioned this (Exod. 23:28; Deut. 7:20). The hornet probably had reference to the terror and panic induced by the Lord that preceded Israel's invasion.[3] The Lord planted Israel in the land, giving them that for which they had not labored.

C. Stipulations: Israel's Obligation (24:14–24)

On the basis of what the Lord had done for them, Joshua rehearsed the obligations of the nation. The word "Now" is spoken in view of what was said in verses 1–13. On the basis of what the Lord did for Israel, the people should "fear the LORD and serve Him." In the suzerainty-vassal treaty there was to be singular obedience and loyalty to the suzerain; hence we find the statement, "Throw away the gods." The loyal vassal could not serve two masters. Joshua appealed to the people to choose whom they would serve. They could serve the gods of Abraham their father from beyond the Euphrates or they could serve the Amorite deities. Joshua was determined to serve the Lord.

In this renewal of the covenant, the people pledged their allegiance to the Lord, even as their fathers had done at the inception of the Mosaic covenant (cf. Exod. 19:8). Their response that the Lord had

---

[3]However, "allies of Israel" is suggested as a possibility (Brown, Driver, and Briggs in *A Hebrew and English Lexicon of the Old Testament*, p. 864. But probably the expression represents the terror that paralyzed the people (cf. 2:9, 11, 24; 5:1; 6:27). Many adopt this view; cf. Davis, *Conquest and Crisis*, p. 89; Bright, "Joshua," p. 669.

brought them up out of the land of Egypt is reminiscent of the opening statement of the Decalogue (Exod. 20:2). They acknowledged the great signs of the Lord (24:15, 18).

Joshua's retort in 24:19 is unusual and reflects an ancient literary device in which a point is accentuated by making it controversial.[4] It was Joshua's way of solemnizing the occasion. He reminded the people of two of the primary attributes of God: His holiness and His jealousy. The term holy (Hebrew, *qadosh*) means God is separate, apart, and thus sacred and holy. He is separate from human infirmity, impurity, and sin.[5] God is also termed a "jealous God." "Jealous" also denotes the zealousness of God in vindicating His name and in judging those who reject His name. Should Israel turn from the Lord and serve foreign gods, God would not forgive them; instead, He would bring chastisement on them.

When the nation once more affirmed their allegiance to the Lord, Joshua reminded them of the significance of their statement. They were witnesses against themselves, that is, should they apostatize, they stood condemned by their own mouths. With that reminder, Joshua exhorted them to put away the foreign gods in their midst (24:23). The statement has possible meanings: 1) It could mean the actual existence of idols among the people. 2) It could refer to idolatry within their hearts. Joshua concluded his appeal by exhorting them to incline their hearts to the Lord (24:23; cf. Deut. 6:5–6).

D. Deposition: The Law's Verification (24:25–28)

In a pattern similar to the Hittite suzerainty-vassal treaty, Joshua "recorded these things in the Book of the Law of God" (24:26). Then Joshua set up a large stone as a witness to the occasion. It is possible that Joshua actually wrote the agreement on a large stone, placing it near the tabernacle, so that all would read it and be reminded of their obligation to God. Having given them the divine directives, Joshua dismissed the people to their own inheritances.

---

[4]Gray, *Joshua, Judges and Ruth*, p. 196.

[5]Brown, Driver, and Briggs, *A Hebrew and English Lexicon of the Old Testament*, p. 872. Payne discusses the three aspects of holiness: "1) Since God the Testator is most 'separate' from His creatures (Ex. 20:19), holiness becomes equivalent to deity (cf. Isa. 5:24; Hab. 3:3). The worship of other gods profanes His *holy* name (Lev. 20:3). 'Holy' is thus synonymous with 'divine'; 'there is none *holy* (uniquely divine) as Yahweh; for there is none beside Thee' (1 Sam. 2:2). . . . 2) God shares His holiness with those who inherit the testament; they, too, are 'separated' unto God (Ex. 19:10, 14; Lev. 20:24). . . . 3) holiness takes on a third meaning: that of conformity to God's moral standards (Lev. 20:7, 8)." Payne, *Theology of the Older Testament*, pp. 123–125.

Chapter 14

Joshua's Death
(Joshua 24:29–33)

A. Burial of Joshua (24:29–31)

As Moses was called a servant of the Lord at the outset of the book (1:1–2), so now at the conclusion Joshua is also termed a servant of the Lord (24:29). When Joshua died at the age of 110, he was buried at his inheritance in the hill country of Ephraim. The faithfulness of Joshua as a servant of the Lord is seen in 24:31. His leadership and influence guided Israel in the worship of the Lord throughout his days and throughout the days of the elders.

B. Burial of Joseph's Bones (24:32)

Although the burial of Joseph's bones probably took place before this time, it is mentioned here in conjunction with Joshua's death to demonstrate the faithfulness of God in bringing Israel into the Promised Land. Joseph had requested burial in the land of Canaan (Exod. 13:19) as an act of faith that God was giving the land as a permanent dwelling place to his posterity.

C. Burial of Eleazar (24:33)

With the death of Eleazar, the contemporary of Joshua, the age of Joshua comes to a conclusion. God had demonstrated His faithfulness in bringing that generation into the land of Canaan—a land that God had promised Abraham and his physical posterity forever (Gen. 12:1–3—a land where Messiah will ultimately establish His kingdom (2 Sam. 7:12–16).

For Further Study

1. Read an article on the attributes of God, noting particularly the qualities of holiness and jealousy, in a book on systematic theology or in a Bible encyclopedia.

2. Analyze Joshua's qualities as a man of God in chapter 24.

3. What does it mean to "fear the Lord" (24:14)? Read an article in a Bible dictionary or encyclopedia on the word "fear."

4. Using the Book of Joshua, suggest as many principles for success as you can.